About This Book

This book is for anyone who works with the opposite sex. Whether you are part of a management team, in human resources, or develop corporate training, this comprehensive guide will give you smart advice, extensive research, and compelling true-to-life case studies. With self-assessments, experiential exercises, quizzes, and insights from a combined seventy years of training and consulting experience in gender communication, this easy-to-follow guide offers compelling advice that will enhance communication between the sexes and affect the bottom line.

Why Is This Topic Important?

The rules for the workplace are constantly changing, and most of us spend more time at work than we do at home. We rely on communication with the opposite sex to get our job done. *The Gender Communication Handbook* was written to clarify some of the many questions about gender and how the rules have changed. This book will help individuals thrive in an increasingly diverse workplace and find a common language. Successful gender communication is a business mandate.

What Can You Achieve with This Book?

This book prepares the trainer with a straightforward, easy-to-understand approach to gender communication. Each chapter presents the background for why men and women communicate the way they do and how to improve it. Easy-to-follow, step-by-step exercises and activities are designed for the new trainer, and more experienced trainers will find this a resource for a novel approach with the latest advances, research, and perspectives on gender communication.

How This Book Is Organized

This book is organized with a chapter on each of the critical gender communication areas. Each chapter contains exercises that include a step-by-step procedure complete with a goal, objectives, setup, materials list, handouts, slides, and debrief. At the conclusion of each chapter is a separate list of action steps for men and women on what they can do to improve communication with the opposite sex.

About Pfeiffer

Pfeiffer serves the professional development and hands-on resource needs of training and human resource practitioners and gives them products to do their jobs better. We deliver proven ideas and solutions from experts in HR development and HR management, and we offer effective and customizable tools to improve workplace performance. From novice to seasoned professional, Pfeiffer is the source you can trust to make yourself and your organization more successful.

Essential Knowledge Pfeiffer produces insightful, practical, and comprehensive materials on topics that matter the most to training and HR professionals. Our Essential Knowledge resources translate the expertise of seasoned professionals into practical, how-to guidance on critical workplace issues and problems. These resources are supported by case studies, worksheets, and job aids and are frequently supplemented with CD-ROMs, websites, and other means of making the content easier to read, understand, and use.

Essential Tools Pfeiffer's Essential Tools resources save time and expense by offering proven, ready-to-use materials—including exercises, activities, games, instruments, and assessments—for use during a training or team-learning event. These resources are frequently offered in looseleaf or CD-ROM format to facilitate copying and customization of the material.

Pfeiffer also recognizes the remarkable power of new technologies in expanding the reach and effectiveness of training. While e-hype has often created whizbang solutions in search of a problem, we are dedicated to bringing convenience and enhancements to proven training solutions. All our e-tools comply with rigorous functionality standards. The most appropriate technology wrapped around essential content yields the perfect solution for today's on-the-go trainers and human resource professionals.

www.pfeiffer.com

Essential resources for training and HR professionals

The Instructor's Guide for
The Gender Communication Handbook by
Audrey Nelson, Ph.D., and Claire Damken Brown, Ph.D.,
includes useful handouts and slides from the book.
The Instructor's Guide is available free online.
If you would like to download a copy, please visit:
www.wiley.com/college/nelsonbrown

The Gender Communication Handbook

Conquering Conversational Collisions Between Men and Women

Audrey Nelson, Ph.D., and Claire Damken Brown, Ph.D.

Pfeiffer
A Wiley Imprint
www.pfeiffer.com

Published by Pfeiffer
An Imprint of Wiley
One Montgomery Street, Suite 1200, San Francisco, CA 94104-4594
www.pfeiffer.com

For additional copies/bulk purchases of this book in the U.S., please contact 800-274-4434.

Pfeiffer books and products are available through most bookstores. To contact Pfeiffer directly, call our Customer Care Department within the U.S. at 800-274-4434, outside the U.S. at 317-572-3985, fax 317-572-4002, or visit www.pfeiffer.com.

Pfeiffer publishes in a variety of print and electronic formats and by print-on-demand. Some material included with standard print versions of this book may not be included in e-books or in print-on-demand. If this book refers to media such as a CD or DVD that is not included in the version you purchased, you may download this material at **http://booksupport.wiley.com**. For more information about Wiley products, visit **www.wiley.com**.

Library of Congress Cataloging-in-Publication Data
Nelson, Audrey.
  The gender communication handbook: conquering conversational collisions between men and women / Audrey Nelson and Claire Damken Brown.
      p. cm.
    Includes bibliographical references and index.
  ISBN 978-1-118-12879-4 (pbk); ISBN 978-1-118-22534-9 (ebk); ISBN 978-1-118-23867-7 (ebk); ISBN 978-1-118-26299-3 (ebk)
1. Interpersonal communication—Sex differences. 2. Interpersonal relations—Sex differences. I. Brown, Claire Damken. II. Title.
  HM1166.N448 2012
  302—dc23
                    2012008102

Acquiring Editor: Matthew C. Davis
Director of Development: Kathleen Dolan Davies
Editor: Elizabeth Forsaith

Editorial Assistant: Michael Zelenko
Manufacturing Supervisor: Becky Morgan

Printed in the United States of America

PB Printing   10 9 8 7 6 5 4 3 2 1

CONTENTS

CHAPTER 3

Gender Conversation Technicalities: Interruptions, Overlapping, and Other Turn-Taking Dilemmas   65

CHAPTER 4

Women, Men, and Unspoken Messages   87

CHAPTER 5

How She and He Listen   135

EXERCISES AND TABLES

Chapter 4: Women, Men, and Unspoken Messages

Chapter 5: How She and He Listen

Chapter 6: Men, Women, and Conflict: Take It Like a Man Versus Nice Girls Don't Do Conflict

Chapter 7: He and She Wired

Chapter 8: Final Thoughts on Reaching Across the Gender Divide

Chapter 9: Example One-Hour Program

Chapter 10: A Half-Day Program

Chapter 11: A Full-Day Program

The field of gender communication has always been a topic of interest and confusion. Most of us realize that men and women have different styles, but we can't put our finger on what component of communication contributed to the mix-up. Because we are unaware of the stylistic differences that exist between men and women, we will often accuse the other sex of having bad intentions, being rude, or being just plain ignorant. We think they are the ones with the problem. But we must start with ourselves. We each have a responsibility in the communication process. We may not be able to control the other person's communication style, but we can manage our own. Our natural tendency is to blame the failure of the relationship on the opposite sex—not productive, but definitely our inclination.

Add to the gender confusion the sheer complexity of the communication process, which involves not only linguistic styles but also unspoken messages—the silent dialogue of nonverbal behaviors—along with such things as the mechanics of the flow of an interaction from interruptions to who has the most airtime in the Monday morning staff meeting, and we wonder how any of us ever connected to close the deal. And as all of us know, where there are people, there is conflict; the mantra "harmony is normal" implies that conflict is abnormal. All workplace environments experience conflict, and it becomes even more of a challenge when we consider the different approaches and styles women and men use to handle it. In addition, the most critical communication skill, listening, has a gender divide that creates havoc at the conference table. Research reveals sex differences in listening is the number one communication complaint registered by both men and women. Finally, the simple daily act of sending an e-mail can backfire if we don't consider the gender nuances in the composition before we hit "send." The risk of ignoring gender differences can be costly and the process of naming them is a business imperative. Pretending there are no sex differences only holds us back and deprives us of the opportunity to be successful and impact the bottom line.

Despite all that's been written, men and women are still misunderstanding each other. Failures in communication can impede career progress, mar relationships, confuse and aggravate daily interactions, and be costly to the organization and our financial well-being. Women and men continue to work together, and we don't see that ending anytime soon. We know men and women bring different leadership and communication styles to the office. We champion differences and believe that men and women can learn from each other. We don't believe women should act like men to succeed, and the business literature on emotional intelligence tells us the new model is not exclusively a male model but rather an androgynous approach. We get into trouble when we believe there is only one way, a rigid approach that can lead to failure. How do we move forward and create a new future of gender communication in the workplace?

In *The Gender Communication Handbook*, internationally recognized gender experts Dr. Audrey Nelson and Dr. Claire Damken Brown explore the intricacies of male-female communication. Audrey and Claire, both Ph.D.'s in communication, bring their collective experience of seventy years of conducting training in gender and diversity for a wide variety of corporations worldwide.

This book goes beyond capturing generalizations. It understands there are individual differences as well as gender similarities. It identifies the ontology and developmental underpinnings of why women and men say and do the things they do; through the process of identifying the sociological and psychological motivations, we minimize defensiveness. This book translates the complexity of gender communication into an easy-to-understand format that trainers can easily convey to their audiences. This is a hands-on systematic guide with how-to action steps for both men and women. It is meant to stimulate participants to question and encourage them to self-monitor their communication behavior through self-assessments, real-life case studies, and experiential exercises. It identifies unsettling questions that go to the core of how we relate to the opposite sex. It's always helpful to understand your gender communication style and how others see you. This book outlines how to build a bigger tool kit for communicating with the opposite sex.

In short, Dr. Nelson and Dr. Brown will help the trainer and corporate audiences decipher the diverse world of gender communication through a practical guide that will enable them to enhance morale and productivity. We must consider new ideas of what it means to be male and female. When women and men embrace the journey by observing gender communication at the office and by questioning the traditional conventions that our culture and society have accepted, we will be better able to reach out to, respect, and understand each other.

ACKNOWLEDGMENTS

We would like to acknowledge with gratitude all the women and men who, over the past thirty-five years, have attended our trainings and trusted us with their workplace stories. In many ways they are equally the authors of this book. Their stories and our experiences from the corporate trenches have encouraged us to continuously move forward to create a more equitable workplace for women and men.

We are professionally grateful for the support and constant guidance we received from our agent, Linda Konner. She is the quintessential professional. A special thank-you to Matthew Davis for his guidance and all the publisher's staff who helped make this book happen.

And most important, to Geoffrey and Larry, for reminding us that gender differences are a good thing.

THE AUTHORS

Audrey Nelson, Ph.D.

Dr. Audrey Nelson is an internationally recognized trainer, keynote speaker, author, and consultant who helps organizations increase their productivity and profitability through winning communication strategies. She specializes in gender communication, conflict management, generational communication, and interpersonal communication skills. She holds a B.A., M.A., and Ph.D. in Communication. She conducted postdoctoral work at Warnborough College in Oxford, England, in gender communication.

Dr. Nelson's professional background includes teaching in the Department of Communication at the University of Colorado at Boulder, San Diego State University, and Southwestern College. Audrey received numerous awards for her teaching, including the most competitive recognition at the University of Colorado at Boulder, the Teaching Excellence Award.

For thirty-five years she has trained and consulted for a wide variety of government and Fortune 50 and 500 companies in forty-nine states, Australia, Great Britain, South Korea, and Canada. Among them are Xcel Energy, Pricewaterhouse Coopers, Cargill, AT&T, Honeywell, Hewlett-Packard, IBM, Upjohn Pharmaceuticals, Pentax, Lockheed

Martin, Johnson & Johnson, U.S. Marine Corps, U.S. Forest Service, and the U.S. Dept. of Justice.

Thirty years ago she cofounded and served as president for the Organization for Research on Women and Communication (ORWAC), which publishes an academic journal dedicated to research on women and communication. ORWAC is a thriving leader of gender research in the United States (www.orwac.com).

Audrey's first book, *You Don't Say: Navigating Nonverbal Communication Between the Sexes* (Prentice Hall, 2004), was published in six languages. She also coauthored *Code Switching: How to Talk So Men Will Listen* (Penguin-Alpha Books, 2009).

Audrey is the gender expert for the *Psychology Today* blog "He Speaks, She Speaks" and for FOX, Denver.

Audrey has produced four CDs of her most requested topics: "He Speaks, She Speaks: What Different Things They Say!" "The Art of Conscious Communication: A Talent for a Technical Age," "Victors Without Victims: Managing Conflict for a Positive Outcome," and "Dealing with Difficult People." For more information about Audrey consult her website at www.AudreyNelson.com.

Claire Damken Brown, Ph.D.

Dr. Claire Damken Brown, founder and president of Damken Brown and Associates, Inc., is a savvy speaker, industry consultant, and seminar leader specializing in diversity and equal employment opportunity strategies, gender communication, sexual harassment prevention, and cultural competency.

A pioneer in the field of diversity, Dr. Brown has twenty-five years of experience in Fortune 50 companies, featuring sixteen years at AT&T and then at Lucent Technologies directing diversity and equal opportunity–related organizations, investigating discrimination cases globally, and training professionals on diversity and legal requirements. She has received numerous awards for her leadership and innovative diversity initiatives. Her doctor's and master's degrees focused on male-female workplace communication.

As a national consultant with various organizations, Claire challenges companies and individuals to look at their organization's systems, interpersonal behaviors, and customer service when integrating diversity and creating a welcoming environment that respects and builds on differences. She is a champion of people achieving their goals in a safe and harassment-free workplace.

Claire volunteers as the diversity director for the Colorado Society for Human Resource Management (COSHRM) State Council. She is an active member of the National Speakers Association, both locally and nationally. As a current adjunct professor at Denver's Metropolitan State College, she engages students in hot topics when teaching the Management Department's workforce diversity and human resources courses.

She is the coauthor of two books: *Conflict and Diversity* (Hampton Press, 1997) and *Code Switching: How to Talk So Men Will Listen*, (Penguin-Alpha Books, 2009). In addition, she has authored several journal and magazine articles. To learn more about Dr. Brown, see her website at www.DamkenBrown.com.

INTRODUCTION: GETTING THE MOST FROM THIS RESOURCE

This book contains eight chapters that each address a critical gender communication skill that men and women require to navigate today's workplace. The topic of gender communication often causes a stir and many sparks to fly. It is a tricky subject for organizations and trainers to address for a number of reasons. For the last four decades, women have entered the workplace in record numbers, changing the dynamics and culture of how we do business. They have contributed to the diversity equation with a different communication style from the historical male model of doing business. There are only two genders—male and female—and, of course, we never think the communication breakdown was our fault, so it is the other gender's fault. The blame game is a common theme you hear around the water cooler: "If he would only listen" or "She just can't get to the point." Finally, communication can take on microinequities: small behaviors enacted on a daily basis that may not be identified easily, but result in hard feelings and a reduction in morale. The subtle and sometimes not-so-subtle exchanges between men and women can make or break a deal and have an impact on the bottom line. For today's workplace, most challenges fall into one or more of these eight dimensions of communication:

How This Book Is Organized

Conducting training in gender communication should start at the beginning with the origins of and most-asked questions participants have about sex differences. Chapter One, "Getting Started: Are Men and Women Just Born Different or Do They Learn to Be Different?" addresses these concerns, identifying the seven most-asked questions, and allows the training to move beyond the classic nature-nurture controversy. Biology is not destiny and participants have a choice in their communication style. The chapter highlight is a self-assessment, The Code-Switching Quotient, a tool designed to identify the participant's ability to implement strategic flexibility by incorporating a more androgynous approach to communication with the opposite sex.

Chapter Two, "He Speaks, She Speaks: What Different Things They Say," moves to the most obvious and familiar form of communication: speech. Specific speech patterns that can incite a communication gap are presented in concrete terms. Diagrams from the anatomy of a question to examples of credibility-robbing qualifiers and disclaimers are illustrated throughout the chapter. An analysis of how everyday speech can undermine our influence or result in being perceived as insensitive by the opposite sex is illustrated through dialogue examples and case studies.

Chapter Three, "Gender Conversation Technicalities: Interruptions, Overlapping, and Other Turn-Taking Dilemmas," identifies the technicalities of communication flow from interruptions, turn taking, and overlapping. Who gets the floor and keeps the floor usually has the most influence. Nothing can frustrate a speaker more than constant interruption, especially if she does not know how to get her turn to talk. The concepts of self-directed and other-oriented people are reviewed in terms of men's and women's communication styles.

Chapter Four, "Women, Men, and Unspoken Messages," addresses the silent dimension of communication; unspoken messages can speak volumes and create off-record behaviors that undermine communication. Years of research have revealed the majority of the meaning of a message is conveyed through nonverbal cues including facial expressions, eye contact, gestures, and much more. This chapter focuses on how to take off-record behavior and put it on record.

Chapter Five, "How She and He Listen," tackles the number one complaint registered by women about men: men don't listen. Of course, men do listen, but they listen differently than women do and maybe not exactly the way women want them to listen. Add to the equation women's more process-oriented style of speaking and men have a challenge trying to listen. Listening is often regarded as the single most important communication skill in the business world. Ask anyone in sales. Not listening can be costly.

Chapter Six, "Men, Women, and Conflict," deals with how women and men handle conflict. A number of erroneous assumptions about conflict and sex differences are addressed. They include how men and women handle anger; stylistic differences such as competition, accommodation, and avoidance; and how control and vulnerability are expressed. Every workplace has conflict; leadership is often judged by how it is handled. This chapter suggests straightforward tips for managing the sex differences in conflict for a productive outcome.

Chapter Seven, "He and She Wired," identifies how men and women compose and use e-mail. In a manner similar to their speech patterns, women will incorporate exclamations, emoticons, and accolades and compose lengthier e-mails. In contrast, men are task-oriented and kings of the one-liner. Both styles serve a purpose but can cause rifts and hard feelings if we are ignorant of these gender nuances.

Chapter Eight, "Final Thoughts on Reaching Across the Gender Divide," summarizes bridging the gender divide with useful tips that stem from the belief that "different but equal" is the mantra we should follow. It acknowledges that gender differences are real and many. Although men and women communicate differently, none of the differences have to be stumbling blocks to performance at work.

Finally, these chapters present action steps for both men and women, training tips that address the relationship of various chapters as well as how to handle difficult topics, sidebars with learning points that add emphasis where needed, case studies derived from work experiences, role-plays, experiential exercises, debriefing sections suitable for minilectures with the latest research and perspectives, and self-assessments. As noted in particular chapters, the chapters themselves may be presented individually as stand-alone programs or *units,* or the chapters may be presented together for a longer program. Alternatively, the trainer may select individual exercises from various chapters to form the content of the trainer's program. Timing and materials for the unit are listed. A chapter *section* groups together similar exercise topics and discussions. A goal, objectives, timing, materials, and setup are listed for each exercise. Chapters Nine, Ten, and Eleven provide example program agendas for one-hour, half-day, and full-day programs. These sample agendas take the exercises from the first eight chapters and provide useful sample agendas for trainers. Both the novice and veteran trainer can use the complete handbook for designing and presenting a training program on gender communication.

A paradigm shift has taken place in the last several decades—the way women and men work has changed forever. This book is about change in the most fundamental form of work: communication. Workforce projections leave no doubt that men and women will be spending time with each other in all capacities and all levels from coworker to CEO. This human capital can be maximized through a working knowledge of hands-on skills to enhance communication between the sexes.

CHAPTER 1

Getting Started

Are Men and Women Just Born Different or Do They Learn to Be Different?

What are little boys made of?
Frogs and snails,
And puppy-dogs' tails;
That's what little boys are made of.
What are little girls made of?
Sugar and spice,
and all that's nice;
That's what little girls are made of.
        —Robert Southey (1820)

Learning Objectives

- Identify the seven most-asked questions about gender communication.

- Create an awareness of the origin of sex differences in communication style.

- Assess personal style and the ability to code switch.

- Understand the importance of adopting an androgynous style to improve communication with the opposite sex.

Introduction

Although we are different, men and women are designed to be allies and can complement each other's limitations; we can fill in the blanks for each other. Conventional wisdom tells us that "our greatest strength is our greatest weakness." We have all witnessed a person rely on a strength in the wrong place or at the wrong time. Ouch! They fail to develop other strengths outside their behavioral repertoire that are more appropriate for the situation. One of the benefits of women and men coming together in the workplace is we can learn from each other. As a case in point, coed teams are usually higher functioning and produce a superior level of results than same-sex groups. Organizations are more effective when they apply both "female" and "male" strengths to maximize the bottom line and reach their goals.

In addition, although men and women often misunderstand each other, most of us don't try to make life difficult for the opposite sex. However, we often mistake and misinterpret each other's actions, words, and feelings. In her book, *In a Different Voice* (1982), Harvard psychologist Carol Gilligan described the problem by claiming that "men and women may speak different languages that they assume are the same . . . creating misunderstandings which impede communication and limit the potential for cooperation" (p. 2). But suggesting that gender communication is problematic is not to imply that all gender communication centers around problems; rather, simply put, it is complicated. Just the act of communication is a multifaceted process. Add gender to the equation and it becomes more complex. Research in psychology, linguistics, sociology, and anthropology demonstrates that sex differences in communication are real. We experience them every day at work and home.

Women and men can be perceived as members of two distinct and separate subcultures within a larger, more general culture. Each subculture has a set of rules, beliefs, behavioral expectations, and verbal and nonverbal symbols. For both men and women, language and nonverbal cues receive reinforcements for employing expected communication styles and sanctions if they should venture into the other's territory. For example, most can fill in the blank: Big boys don't (cry), take it like a (man), and boys will be (boys).

In addition, this is not about sexuality. Sex is your biological determination and an unchangeable fact at birth (although in adulthood, some people decide to change their sex). Gender refers to and is created through communication; gender is learned communication behaviors. Many people think biological sex and constructed gender are the same thing. They are not. Bate (1992) distinguishes sex as referring to biologically determined, innate features and treated as permanent fact. She describes gender as socially learned behaviors, treated as behavioral ideals to achieve and prescribe (p. 5).

> Women and men can be perceived as members
> of two distinct and separate subcultures.

Gender issues in communication begin at birth and are part of your life until you die. They never go away. For example, we know that before you draw your first breath, discussions have taken place indicating a preference for one sex or the other. The color and design of the nursery is gender specific and now the stage is set. As early as two to three years old, children learn their sex and the attending gender expectations. Only for a brief time do children engage in mixed-gender play and dress before they relinquish the gender behavior of the other sex. A boy insists on wearing barrettes in his hair and a girl refuses to wear a dress or her black patent shoes. It's Barbie and play makeup for her and trucks and Transformers for him.

A girl can be a "tomboy" or assume more boy behaviors, and it is still within the acceptable range among adults and her peer group. However, a boy will be admonished as a "sissy" for displaying any female behaviors; he is a wimp. Boys may be dissuaded from developing an understanding of the feminine experience by the off-putting messages about femininity. He cannot explore femininity because it is highly taboo. One could argue that because there seems to be a broader range of acceptance for girls to be able to explore and assume boy behaviors, they have an advantage. She can cross over and he cannot. The entrenchment and rigidity of masculinity begins and stays with him for life. Femininity is not so inflexible.

Timing for Unit

45 minutes to 1 hour

Materials for Unit

Handouts, chart paper and easel, markers

Slides 1.1 through 1.5

Section 1: Introduction to Gender: It's Complicated

Exercise 1.1. Warm-Up Exercise:
The Seven Most-Asked Questions

Goal

Identify the most-asked questions about gender communication.

Objectives

- Create an awareness of predispositions and commonly held beliefs regarding gender communication.

- Discuss the range of attitudes toward gender communication.

- Define the origin and nature of gender differences.

Timing of Exercise

15–20 minutes

Materials

Handout: The Seven Most-Asked Questions, chart paper and easel, markers

Slide 1.1.

Setup

☐ Conduct this exercise in dyads and then process it with the entire group or organize it in groups of five to eight members, where each member shares his or her response, and then process it with the entire group.

☐ The content for the handout is the same as the content on slide 1.1. Distribute the handout.

☐ Solicit the group for three or four of the seven questions with the entire group participating. The trainer presents the responses to the remaining questions. In other words, the group can dictate what questions they are most interested in to begin the discussion; then the trainer supplements the answers to the remaining questions.

☐ Ask the group for the questions that received the most attention or debate. Question 1 is usually selected most often, followed by question 6.

Debrief

1. How did men and women acquire their communication styles? Are we just born that way, or did we learn them? Is it a question of nature or nurture?

   • Ask for a show of hands of participants who believe sex differences are primarily a result of nurture or environmental influences or if they are learned.

   • Then ask how many participants believe that sex differences are inherited by nature.

   • Finally, ask how many think sex differences are a result of both nature and nurture. Most people are aware that sex differences are a combination of both environmental influences and genetic predispositions.

Slide 1.1

The Seven Most-Asked Questions

1. How did men and women acquire their communication styles? Are we just born that way, or did we learn them? Is it a question of nature or nurture?

2. Which communication style is better: male or female?

3. Is gender really that important in defining the way people interact with each other?

4. Can men and women learn to change and adapt their styles? Haven't we been this way forever? How do you expect us to change?

5. Are there individual differences, as well as gender differences?

6. Who acts as though they're responsible for effective gender communication: women or men?

7. Haven't things changed in gender relationships?

Source: Nelson, 2004, p. 17.

Most people are aware that sex differences are a combination of both environmental influences and genetic predispositions.

- Ask the group to provide examples of influences of both nature and nurture. Nature or inherited biological examples would include that male and female brains are wired differently. Hormones also affect behavior. For example, boys are genetically programmed to be more aggressive than girls; girls are genetically programmed to be more nurturing than boys. Finally, girls acquire language sooner than boys, who tend to be better in spatial-relations ability. This is the "nature" part of the equation. And remember, biology is not destiny.

- Nurture is also a part of the gender equation. We are socialized through being rewarded by adults for gender-appropriate behavior when we are children. Children imitate adult role models and are influenced by peers. Other influences include television, popular music, Hollywood, and social networking. Remember, the average child is in front of a screen (texting, e-mail, TV, computer) approximately six hours a day. Ask the group to reflect on messages they received from their parents, teachers, peers, or a coach on what it meant to be a boy or a girl. Solicit the group to share some examples.

- Ask the group members if they can think of any other double standards for behaviors that might have been sanctioned for one gender but not the other.

2. Which communication style is better: male or female?

- As the saying goes, "There are no dumb questions." But from the perspective of communication, this is the wrong question to ask. No one gender has the edge on a better communication style. Both women and men are unique in their styles, and each brings a different perspective and skill set to the table. The more correct question to ask is, "What style best fits the situation?" The mantra in communication is, "Communication is context bound." The context or situation dictates what kind of communication style should be used;

that is, a successful communicator has the plasticity and flexibility in his or her communication style to be able to adapt to the particular needs of a situation. Some contexts may call for empathic listening, such as when a coworker announces they were just denied a promotion. This is typically a more feminine style. However, a situation where a brief, to-the-point summary is required is more typical of men's linguistic style. Some encounters call for a synergistic blend of styles or an androgynous approach.

3. Is gender really that important in defining the way people interact with each other? Yes, gender is a predictor of communication style. The distinction between male and female is perhaps the most obvious, visible, and dramatic subdivision within our species. An abundance of empirical and theoretical literature documents sex differences in behavioral realms, brain functioning, cognitive skills, peer relations, and hormonal makeup.

   • Many demographic variables affect communication. Solicit the audience for examples. The most common factors are age, socioeconomic status, race, and cultural identification. Gender is one of the most significant variables affecting the choices we make in how we communicate.

4. Can men and women learn to change and adapt their styles? Haven't we been this way forever? How do you expect us to change?

   • Yes, both men and women can change and have the ability to adapt and modify their communication styles. This is a shared equal opportunity. Change is a choice. And as stated earlier, biology is not destiny. Yes, men and women can learn to change, and this training is about how you can change and alter or modify your communication behaviors to be more successful with the opposite sex. Some participants may express a betrayal of self: "Well, this just isn't me." We are always evolving and change is inevitable. True, some people are more open and receptive to change than others. And the goal of this training is to evolve into a better, new, and improved communicator. The more someone can expand his or her communication behavioral repertoire, the more successful he or she will be.

5. Are there individual differences, as well as gender differences?

- In addition to gender differences in communication, there are also individual differences. It is common to hear a female participant say, "Wow, I identify more with the male characteristics of communication style." Or a male supervisor exclaims, "You have not met my female assistant. She is a bulldog." On the home front, people will disclose that they have almost swapped gender styles in their marriage. A woman will remark, "I think I am the man on my team, because I am direct and to the point, have no problem putting conflict on the table, and am not the best at empathizing."

  We are all unique and don't always fit neatly into the gender box. Gender is one aspect of who we are, and personality traits can certainly play a role in defining our communication style. Social psychologist Douglas Kenrick and his colleagues suggest that "stereotyping is a cognitively inexpensive way of understanding others: By presuming that people are like members of their group, we avoid the effortful process of learning about them as individuals" (Kenrick, Neuberg, & Cialdini, 2002, p. 339).

6. Who acts as though they're responsible for effective gender communication: women or men?

- Traditionally, women have assumed the role of social maintenance. They take care of people and relationships. Women can "read" feelings and are usually better able to empathize. There is also a societal expectation that because women are the nurturers, the moms, they automatically come equipped to soothe hurt feelings and offer counsel. At work, a woman is often called the "office mom."

*Traditionally, women have assumed
the role of social maintenance.*

7. Haven't things changed in gender relationships?

    • Of course things have changed. But have we arrived? No. Listen
      to the watercooler talk and pick up the newspaper. Old
      attitudes are pretty firmly entrenched and still lurking in the
      hallway and evident in the Monday morning staff meeting.
      Some attitudes are subtle and others not so subtle.

      Often people assume that with close to four decades of women
      having entered the workforce, we've arrived. Haven't we given
      enough attention to this gender problem at work? Aren't we
      beating a dead horse?

      Bill, a manager at a factory location of Lucent Technologies,
      recently suggested, "When I began here as an engineer thirty-
      five years ago, there wasn't a single woman in my department.
      Now a woman heads it. Women are everywhere. Things have
      changed!"

      You have to admit that he has a point. Twenty years ago, it was
      easier to identify inequities between men and women because
      there were far fewer females in the workplace, especially in
      senior positions. Overtly, it seems as if we've altered our actions
      to meet the new requirements of corporate America, which
      often has zero tolerance toward any communication inequities,
      such as ignoring women, hoarding power and information, or
      excluding them from networks.

      But Bill mistakenly equates the larger number of women
      holding jobs with equitable treatment. Just because there are
      more professional and working women doesn't yet mean that
      they have arrived, or that attitudes toward them have changed.
      Men still dominate senior executive and CEO positions of
      Fortune 500 companies, and they still make more money than
      women, even for the same jobs.

Although outwardly we all know how to behave, internally certain mind-sets still prevail at work. Occasionally that inner, unspoken perception that affects women reveals itself in a spontaneous remark or gesture. Attitudes drive behavior, and attitudes are not all that plastic or flexible. In spite of everything, they're tough to change.

Finally, there is a great debate on who is doing the most changing. Men complain that they have had to make adjustments because now they are in "mixed" company. It cramps their style. Women complain that they have had to change to meet the male standard of behavior in the workplace. Men set the rules and women must follow them. Actually, it is vital for both sexes to understand each other. Both will benefit from the knowledge of gender communication style differences and how they affect the way the sexes are perceived. And remember, most men and women have goodwill toward each other. They are just lacking knowledge. Intent is not enough, and impact is the bottom line and the measure of successful communication. Once the obstacles are identified, they can be overcome.

Section 1: Introduction to Gender: It's Complicated (continued)

Exercise 1.2.
Case Study: Big Boys Don't Cry

Goal

Provide an example of a sex-role message and the influence of "nurture."

Objectives

- Understand how boys and girls learn sex roles.

- Create an awareness of the unintentional dual prescriptions of appropriate and sanctioned behaviors for boys and girls.

Timing of Exercise

10–15 minutes total:

5 minutes to read the case study and talk in small groups

10 minutes to hear responses from each group or sample of groups

Materials

Handout: Case Study: Big Boys Don't Cry, chart paper and easel, markers

Setup

☐ Explain the process to the large group.

☐ The content for the handout includes the case study and questions.

☐ Ask the participants to read the handout with the case study and questions.

☐ Address each question with the entire class and ask for the individual group answers.

Case Study: Big Boys Don't Cry

Audrey's eldest child, Alexandra, and son, Armand, are four years apart and had the same teacher for second grade. During parent-teacher conferences, the issue of crying was brought to Audrey's attention. Armand's teacher shared that he would occasionally cry when he was frustrated with a work assignment or when he chose the wrong answer and was corrected. Audrey asked the teacher if Alexandra would also occasionally cry when she was a student in her class. The teacher replied that she did. Armand's crying required parent notification and was an issue. In contrast, Alexandra's crying was a nonissue and acceptable.

Source: Copyright © 2012 by Audrey Nelson and Claire Damken Brown.

Questions

1. Is there a double standard for crying?

2. Is there an implied sanction for boys' crying?

3. What kind of implication does this have for socialization? What is the message?

4. Do we want our children to be stuck in a gender box?

Section 2: What Do Women and Men Really Think of Each Other?

Exercise 1.3. One Thing I Wish the Opposite Sex Would Change in Their Communication Style

Goal

Create an awareness of challenges communicating with the opposite sex.

Objectives

- Identify specific communication skills that both women and men could improve.

- Discuss shared perceptions or emerging themes from the group.

Timing of Exercise

10–15 minutes

Materials

Colored paper with four different colors, chart paper and easel, markers

Slide 1.2

Setup

☐ Conduct this exercise with small-group discussions and then process it in the large group or do this with the large group only.

☐ Distribute colored sheets of paper (to encourage anonymity).

☐ Ask the participants to respond to the question, "What is one communication behavior you wish the opposite sex would change?" One or two sentences are sufficient.

☐ Participants do not sign their names.

☐ Participants must indicate whether they are referring to men or women; for example, "I wish women would speak more to the point."

☐ Ask participants to fold their colored paper into a paper airplane.

☐ When they are finished, ask the participants to stand up to wait for the cue from the instructor to throw the airplane into the air (this is done simultaneously in one group).

☐ On the count of three, have the participants throw their airplanes into the air and then each retrieve one.

☐ Break up the large group into smaller groups of five to eight.

☐ Allow two to three minutes for everyone to share what is written on their respective airplanes. Each group gets to choose one to share with the larger group discussion.

☐ Solicit the group for the communication behaviors that received the most attention or debate.

Debrief

In research conducted by Audrey Nelson (2004) with one hundred men and women across the United States, she asked four questions (see slide 1.2). The responses to these questions revealed the respondents' self-perception, as well as their awareness of how their gender communicates with the opposite sex. A major finding was that there was no debate: Men and women had significantly shared views of their own and the opposite sex's weaknesses and strengths in communication—and these are weaknesses and strengths that seem to have been written about since time immemorial in the media and portrayed by Hollywood (p. 20).

Slide 1.2

Four Questions on Gender Communication

- What do you feel is the greatest strength in women's communication?

- What do you feel is the greatest strength in men's communication?

- What do you feel is the biggest weakness in women's communication?

- What do you feel is the biggest weakness in men's communication?

Source: Copyright © 2012 by Audrey Nelson and Claire Damken Brown.

Men revealed their weaknesses in communication as failure to read nonverbal cues, trying to solve women's problems ("Mr. Fix It"), inability to stay focused on what people are saying, lack of expressing their emotions, and poor listening habits. More important, according to the study, men perceive women to have the edge in the interpersonal arena. Men perceive that this "division of labor" is an accepted norm. Men admit they are "out to lunch" when it comes to that sensitivity (pp. 22–23).

Men perceive women to have the
edge in the interpersonal arena.

Women identified men's weaknesses as assuming they know what you are going to say before you finish. They interrupt the conversation and seldom allow people to finish their thoughts. Furthermore, women claimed men listen to what others say, but they do not actually hear and absorb the right information. They are unable to really empathize with the other person's feelings; they're too focused on trying to fix the problem. Men tend to zero in on only one aspect: the verbal (p. 22).

On the positive side, the majority of women's comments indicated that they believe men are direct, speak with confidence, and get to the point. According to the women surveyed, men's strongest areas include forcefulness, credibility, and control (p. 22).

The men surveyed identified women's skills as the ability to make observations of subtle nuances, usually being more thoughtful and sensitive to other people's communication and being good empathic listeners (p. 24).

When women were asked about their strengths, they most frequently reported listening, empathy, and the ability to express emotions. A woman claimed that they "put the human element into conversation: caring, compassion, interest in the other person." Moreover, in critiquing their own communication style, women admitted to being overly emotional and indirect. Many expressed a desire to present themselves in a more credible way (p. 23).

Section 3: Transcending Gender: The Androgynous Answer

Exercise 1.4. The Code-Switching Quotient

Goal

Examine an androgynous approach to gender communication.

Objectives

- Create an awareness of the continuum and range of masculinity and femininity.

- Identify how an androgynous approach can enhance communication between the sexes.

Timing of Exercise

15–20 minutes

Materials

Handout: Code-Switching Quotient (located at the end of this chapter), chart paper and easel, markers

Slides 1.3 through 1.5

Setup

☐ Conduct this exercise with small-group discussion and then process it in the large group, or do this with the large group only.

☐ Distribute the handout.

☐ Ask the participants to assess themselves on the thirty communication traits.

☐ Instruct the participants to use the workplace as the context (not home or outside of work).

☐ Encourage the participants to go with their "first gut-level response" and not to mull over their responses.

☐ The participants must respond to all thirty characteristics; none can be omitted.

☐ Ask the participants to complete the scoring as instructed in the questionnaire.

☐ Break up the class into coed groups of five to eight.

☐ Allow five to ten minutes for participants to share their final Code-Switching Quotient.

☐ Ask for a show of hands for participants who had a final score in one of the four categories shown in slide 1.3.

Slide 1.3

Code-Switching Quotient Total Key

140–150 = Code-Switcher SUPERSTAR

120–139 = EFFECTIVE Code Switcher

99–119 = ROOM FOR Code-Switching IMPROVEMENT

30–98 = DANGER ZONE: Code-Switching Class Required

Source: Copyright © 2012 by Audrey Nelson and Claire Damken Brown.

Debrief

The Code-Switching Quotient (CSQ) is a descriptive instrument designed to assess the degree and incorporation of both masculine and feminine communication behaviors. CSQ scores will vary according to an individual's station in life and position at work. Almost everyone's style of communication changes according to the person's current work life and personal situation.

- Ask the participants if they can identify CSQ traits that are more characteristically employed by men or women. The following are usually masculine communication traits: 1, 2, 3, 4, 5, 6, 7, 9, 12, 15, 20, 21, 25, 26, and 27. The feminine communication traits are: 8, 10, 13, 14, 16, 17, 18, 19, 22, 23, 28, 29, and 30. *Note:* Traits 11 and 24 are considered "gender neutral."

- Ask the audience if anyone feels their CSQ score would have been different ten years ago or with a former employer. This will emphasize the changing nature of our communication styles.

Slide 1.4

Androgyny

The word *androgyny* derives from a combination of the Greek words *andros,* meaning man, and *gyne,* meaning woman (as in the prefix to *gyne*cology).

Source: Copyright © 2012 by Audrey Nelson and Claire Damken Brown.

Communication professors Virginia Richmond, James McCroskey and Steven Payne (1991) define an androgynous person as "one who can associate with both masculine and feminine characteristics. In terms of psychological gender orientation, this type of individual is able to adapt to a variety of roles by engaging in either responsive or assertive behaviors, depending on the situation" (p. 35).

Androgyny is the ability to genderflex or code switch. *Code switching* is a term derived from linguistics and refers to "the knowledge of two cultures or languages and readily swapping between them as you communicate" (C. Brown & Nelson, 2009, p. viii). Judith Tingley (1994), a psychologist, defined *genderflex* as the ability to "temporarily use communication behaviors typical of the other gender in order to increase potential for influence" (p. 39).

The word *androgyny* derives from a combination
of the Greek words *andros*, meaning man,
and *gyne*, meaning woman.

The famous American journalist and critic of American life and culture H. L. Mencken (1920) said, "Neither sex, without some fertilization of the complimentary characteristics of the other, is capable of the highest reaches of human endeavor." Author Amy Bloom (2002) makes this point about the range or continuum of masculinity and femininity: "Our mistake is to think that the wide range of humanity represents aberration when in fact it represents just what it is: a range. Nature is not two little notes—masculine or feminine—on a child's flute. Nature is more like Aretha Franklin: vast, magnificent, capricious—occasionally hilarious and infinitely varied" (p. 69).

Swiss psychiatrist Carl Jung (2009) talked of the two parts of our personalities: the anima and the animus. Chinese philosophy has taught us about the masculine and feminine: the Yin and Yang. Jung believed that in order to have a whole personality, the goal of the person is to integrate the side opposite to their gender. Therefore, men must integrate their anima, or feminine side, and women must integrate their animus, or masculine side.

Today's workplace is a different world. Due to shifts in business operating environments, such as globalization and increased competition, leadership is increasingly moving away from an outdated "command-and-control" masculine model focused only on the task, toward a more blended team-oriented approach that understands the value and bottom-line profit of interpersonal skills and emotional intelligence. It is forcing both men and women to adopt each other's strongpoints. But outdated, entrenched sex-role perceptions and expectations are still embedded in some corporate cultures. We have all heard someone remark that a strong and vigorous woman was "pushy" or an empathetic and nurturing man was a "wimp." Think about the terms you have heard in the media: *metrosexual* and *girlie men*. Both men and women who strongly identify and fit into traditional gender stereotype styles of communication experience more anxiety and have lower self-esteem. They are not successful with others, especially the opposite sex. Extremely feminine women often exhibit dependency and self-denial and harbor disappointment. Extremely masculine men risk being perceived as rude, arrogant, and exploitative. In contrast, androgynous people tend to be characterized as more creative, able to get along with almost anyone, and less anxious. These are the people we feel good being around.

Both women and men are expected to be partners at work. When the strengths of both sexes' traditional styles are respected, and wide variations are allowed in fitting the behavior to the circumstance, then the workplace benefits and reaps the rewards of an inclusive or androgynous style. Behavioral flexibility is the key to effective communication strategies in all organizational settings.

Behavioral flexibility is the key
to effective communication strategies
in all organizational settings.

---

training tip

The concept of androgyny will occasionally receive some push back, especially from men.

As a facilitator, be aware that some men may disagree with the concept and value of androgyny. Men who may be more invested in "masculinity" and the concept of being "macho" may disagree with the recommended value of using an androgynous style of communication. Generally fewer women prefer to maintain a feminine-only style. Most women seem to agree on and find value in using an androgynous communication style.

Emphasize that the concept is not about men becoming women or women becoming men. *Vive la difference!* We don't want to all be alike. It is our differences that make for better outcomes.

Unfortunately, the concepts of feminine and masculine are often experienced by most people as two separate constructs, and they work to attain a gender ideal, despite its being detrimental to them. Ask for a show of hands for anyone who has ever felt torn between trying to attain a gender ideal and wishing they could escape the limitations. Ask for anyone to volunteer a short personal example.

Communication works to reinforce and re-create gender, often intentionally and sometimes unintentionally, in everyday life.

Slide 1.5
Characteristics of Code Switchers

An individual who can code switch and has an androgynous style is characterized as follows:

- A man who can develop interpersonal skills and still have the ability to be strong and exercise his power.

- A woman who can be assertive and still be described as sensitive to others' needs.

- Women and men who retain their natural strengths and do not need to suppress them.

- Men and women who can learn and practice new ways of responding to others.

- Women and men who have the ability to self-monitor, that is, to assess accurately the impact that their behavior has on others, and therefore who will be more successful in their communication with the opposite sex.

Source: Copyright © 2012 by Audrey Nelson and Claire Damken Brown.

Refer to this book's Additional Instruments and Training Tools section, Chapter One, for other resources on understanding gender socialization.

CODE-SWITCHING QUOTIENT

Directions:

The following thirty statements are about code-switching communication. Read each statement carefully. Then, using the response key, decide how often you practice the communication described in each statement. Record your answers by checking the appropriate boxes. As you respond, your frame of reference should be your communication behavior during group and one-on-one conversations at work.

Response Key:

Almost Always, Most of the Time, Some of the Time, Occasionally, Almost Never

Statements	Almost Always	Most of the Time	Some of the Time	Occasionally	Almost Never
1. When I ask someone to do something, I refrain from using lots of unnecessary words and I am direct in my request.					
2. When I speak to people at work, I am not excessive in my use of adjectives (words that describe).					
3. I can express my disappointment and dissatisfaction directly and clearly to others.					
4. I can say no to requests.					
5. I can leave out the details and get to the point.					

Source: Developed by Audrey Nelson, Ph.D., and Claire Damken Brown, Ph.D. Copyright © 2012 by Audrey Nelson, Ph.D., and Damken Brown and Associates, Inc.

	Statements	Almost Always	Most of the Time	Some of the Time	Occasionally	Almost Never
6.	I am not offended or hurt when someone does not agree with my ideas.					
7.	I manage my emotions in the office when I am upset due to work issues.					
8.	My communication shows that I nurture and support others.					
9.	If I am interrupted, I actively seek to get the floor back.					
10.	I tend to let the other person complete their thoughts without interrupting them before I respond with my comments.					
11.	I have the flexibility to change my communication style to fit the needs and requirements of the person(s) with whom I am talking.					
12.	I am comfortable questioning or debating my colleague during a conversation.					
13.	I use head nodding and statements of acknowledgment (e.g.,"uh-huh" or "yes") when listening.					

Source: Developed by Audrey Nelson, Ph.D., and Claire Damken Brown, Ph.D. Copyright © 2012 by Audrey Nelson, Ph.D., and Damken Brown and Associates, Inc.

Statements	Almost Always	Most of the Time	Some of the Time	Occasionally	Almost Never
14. I use greetings in my e-mails (e.g., "dear," "hello").					
15. I am comfortable using a goal-oriented style when needed.					
16. I make sure everyone has had an opportunity to contribute in meetings.					
17. I balance my needs with the needs of others.					
18. I incorporate gratitude ("thanks") and affirmation or acknowledgment ("I appreciate your help") in e-mails.					
19. When interacting with others, I listen to both the spoken words and unspoken feelings.					
20. I speak in an assertive manner.					
21. I usually don't use emoticons in business e-mails.					
22. I am good at empathizing with people's feelings.					
23. I am perceived by others as a good listener.					
24. I make sure my nonverbal message (actions, expressions) is congruent with my verbal message (words).					

	Statements	Almost Always	Most of the Time	Some of the Time	Occasionally	Almost Never
25.	When I speak it generally sounds like a declaration of fact and authoritative.					
26.	I can engage in conflict.					
27.	I have no problem setting boundaries.					
28.	I use eye contact to signal support.					
29.	I am sensitive to how my message affects others.					
30.	I read nonverbal cues that are exchanged in an interaction.					
	Total					

Interpreting Your Code-Switching Quotient

You have just completed the Code-Switching Quotient. Add the number checked in each category of your questionnaire and multiply as noted below. Then add your points and see the suggested interpretation of the total score.

Almost always   ____ × 5 = ____

Most of the time   ____ × 4 = ____

Some of the time   ____ × 3 = ____

Occasionally   ____ × 2 = ____

Almost never   ____ × 1 = ____

TOTAL POINTS   = ____

Total Key:

140–150 = Code-Switching SUPERSTAR

120–139 = EFFECTIVE Code Switching

99–119 = ROOM FOR Code-Switching IMPROVEMENT

30–98 = DANGER ZONE: Code-Switching Class Required

Source: Developed by Audrey Nelson, Ph.D., and Claire Damken Brown, Ph.D. Copyright © 2012 by Audrey Nelson, Ph.D., and Damken Brown and Associates, Inc.

CHAPTER 2

He Speaks, She Speaks
What Different Things They Say

When I talk about women's and men's characteristic ways of speaking, I always emphasize that both styles make sense and are equally valid in themselves.

—Deborah Tannen (1994, p. 23)

Learning Objectives

- Distinguish between popular myths and the reality of sex differences in speech style.

- Identify examples of women's polite forms of speech.

- Identify examples of men's task-oriented forms of speech.

- Examine the underpinnings of gender linguistic styles.

- Create the awareness that one style is not preferred over another style.

- Identify strategies, such as an androgynous approach or code switching, to enhance speech communication between the sexes.

Introduction

We know women and men are speaking the same language, but our conversations are filled with land mines of misunderstanding—same language and lots of confusion. This equal-opportunity fallout from sex differences in conversational style can have unequal consequences for both women and men at work. Men and women have been taught to use language differently since they uttered their first words. Women use language as a social medium; that is, for women, communication is a mechanism for social maintenance, relationship building, and creating bonds. For her, language serves the purpose of connecting. In contrast, men use language primarily to exchange information and for implementing tasks. However, women employ speech strategies, such as tag questions, qualifiers, and hedging, as though they are requesting, not commanding. These speech strategies are viewed as more polite and "other" oriented in contrast to men's patterns of speech. A power imbalance exists. People, usually women, in lower positions or who are perceived in a power-down position use politeness as a strategy for gaining and maintaining favor. People in power positions are not compelled to be polite and they can be more direct (Borisoff and Merrill, 1992).

P. Brown and Levinson (1978) suggest that members of dominated and muted groups, including women, tend to engage in politeness strategies that affirm commonality when speaking with each other. They claim that politeness strategies based on avoidance and deference are more commonly used when communicating with dominant groups. However, although women may feel unevenly matched at times, it is important to emphasize that their more tentative style can be judged incorrectly and interpreted as being unsure, uninformed, or unacquainted with the subject. Not true.

Exploring the motivations that underlie speech style helps us understand why men and women talk the way they do. Through this understanding we lessen the misunderstandings. Men and women employ different linguistic strategies and often have different goals.

One goal is not superior to the other, just different. By questioning these patterns and knowing what the desired outcome is, we might not be so offended and may develop alternative communication techniques that are more successful with getting our message across to the opposite sex.

Timing for Unit

45 minutes to 1 hour

Materials for Unit

Handouts, chart paper and easel, markers

Slides 2.1 through 2.9

Section 1: Talk the Talk: Facts and Fiction About Sex Differences in Speech Communication

Exercise 2.1. Talk the Talk: Facts and Fiction About Sex Differences in Speech Communication

Goal

Identify some myths about sex differences in speech communication.

Objectives

- Create an awareness of popular myths and stereotypes in speech patterns.

- Explore and identify what purpose speech patterns serve.

Timing of Exercise

20–25 minutes total:

8–10 minutes to complete true/false questions and discuss them with the group

10–15 minutes to get comments from individuals or a sample of the groups

Materials

Handout: Talk the Talk: Myths About Sex Differences in Speech Communication, chart paper and easel, markers

Slide 2.1

Setup

☐ The content for the handout is the same as the content on slide 2.1. Distribute the handout.

☐ Begin with a staccato stand-up exercise (dyads are with each other two to three minutes) for the first three true/false questions and then transition to a seated group discussion for the remaining seven true/false questions.

☐ Instruct the participants to stand up, and inform them they will not need anything (no workbooks or pens).

☐ Tell them to take up the entire room and to push their chairs into the tables to allow for more room and freedom of movement.

☐ The first three true/false questions will be answered in dyads and take only two minutes with each of the three different partners. In other words, each person will have three different partners with a different true/false question for each exchange.

☐ Have the participants pick their partners. Encourage them to choose someone they do not know or do not know very well.

☐ If you have an uneven number of participants, one group can have three members. Participants will stand for the entire exercise (answering the first three true/false questions).

☐ State the first true/false question: Women talk more than men do. Instruct them to answer true/false and explain why they believe it is true/false. Advise them that they have two minutes.

☐ After two minutes tell them to stop, and ask the large group who said true and why. Then ask who said false and why. Spend three to four minutes processing the answers with the large group.

Slide 2.1

TALK THE TALK: Myths About Sex Differences in Speech Communication

Indicate whether the following statements are true/false. Circle your choice:

1. True/false: Women talk more than men do.

2. True/false: Women usually select the topic of discussion.

3. True/false: Men incorporate more adjectives and adverbs in their speech.

4. True/false: Men speak more in declarative sentences.

5. True/false: Women engage in rapport talk trying to "connect" with others.

6. True/false: Men focus on "safe" topics, such as work and sports.

7. True/false: Women are direct with requests.

8. True/false: Men apologize more than women.

9. True/false: Women incorporate more indirect verb forms (might, would, or could).

10. True/false: Men are self-effacing in their speech.

☐ After the large-group discussion, instruct the participants to find new partners for a different true/false question.

☐ Continue the same pattern with the second true/false question: Women usually select the topic of discussion, and the third true/ false: Men incorporate more adjectives and adverbs in their speech.

☐ After the group has completed the first three true/false questions, ask the participants to go back to their respective seats, and solicit the large group for answers to the remaining seven true/false questions.

Debrief

1. Women talk more than men do.

   False. A popular myth and brunt of jokes is that women are the talkers; women talk more than men do. We hear terms such as Chatty Cathy or yakkity-yak when referring to women and how they can go on and on.

   Actually, men get the floor more often, and when they get it, they keep it longer. Women are also the recipients of more interruptions. One of the most extensive studies was conducted by linguists Don Zimmerman and Candace West (1975), which demonstrated that men interrupted women much more than they interrupted other men and far more often than women interrupted either men or women (96 percent, compared with 4 percent). This conversational inequality has been slowly changing. There is new evidence that women are providing support to other women when they are interrupted, often saying something like, "I'd like to hear the rest of her idea." In addition, rather than becoming silent when men interrupt them, more women are becoming assertive and requesting to finish (Bate, 1992). Mindell (1995) suggests that women build a repertoire of "polite ways to say shut up." These are some of her recommendations:

   Please . . .

   Just a moment . . .

I'm not finished . . .

Kindly hold the remarks till I'm done . . . (p. 105).

Additional strategies might include, "I would like to finish without interruption" or "John, I am almost done, please let me finish."

A final variable that affects who talks more is overlapping. Overlapping is when one person talks over another person; two people are talking at the same time. Bate says the motivation for men's tendency to overlap is related to the viewpoint of "dominance and power" (1992, p. 98). In contrast, when women overlap, it usually serves the purpose of supporting or expressing interest. Women seldom overlap to assert control, but rather to build relationship and connection, revealing a more cooperative approach to conversation rather than a competitive one.

Taken together, these variables contribute to women speaking less than men do. Some say women talk too much. If you have worked in Congress, you know that the filibuster was invented by men. At your next Monday morning staff meeting, take notice. Who is really doing more of the talking? Who is getting more of the airtime: men or women?

training tip

Consult Chapter Three, "Gender Conversation Technicalities," for a more comprehensive discussion of the mechanics of turn taking, overlapping, and interruption and the relation to speech length.

Challenge the participants to keep a check list of who talked (what gender) and for how long in the next Monday morning staff meeting. It might provide some insight to report the informal data at the next meeting. If that data suggests both men and women take roughly the same number of turns and speak almost, on average, for the same length of time, it is an equitable exchange.

2. Women usually select the topic of discussion.

   False. Selecting the topic of conversation sets the stage and directs the course of the interaction. It can also have persuasive implications and enhance credibility. In a sense, it is taking charge of the exchange. Generally, men will take the lead and initiate the topics of conversation.

   Generally, men will take the lead and initiate the topics of conversation.

   ---

3. Men incorporate more adjectives and adverbs in their speech.

   False. Women incorporate a more descriptive speech style, which includes the use of more adjectives and adverbs. Men are often more empirical in their speech style; that is, most men are more analytical and literal.

   Examples of the more frequent use of intensive adverbs employed by women are: very, terribly, quite, such, awfully, and just. A man might say, "That was nice." A woman might say, "That was awfully nice." Adverbs can convey a less forceful or credible message. They have the effect of weakening speech. Compare "I really want that job" to "I want that job." Or "She had the very best office" to "She had the best office."

   Adjectives are words that describe and might include lovely, sweet, precious, wonderful, charming, or cute. They also include color distinctions employed by women such as ecru, chartreuse, lavender, or taupe. Try to imagine a man using any of these words. Taken together, the more excessive use of adverbs and adjectives can trivialize women's speech. Men often think of matters such as color distinction and excessive description as trivial and unimportant.

4. Men speak more in declarative sentences.

   True. Men not only speak more frequently in declarative sentences, but also their pitch goes down at the end of the sentence, signaling finality and conclusiveness. The result is often a persuasive, all-knowing tone that should not be questioned. This combination of the verbal (declarative sentence) with the nonverbal (deeper pitch at the end of the sentence) is a rhetorical tool employed by men that leaves the listener believing there is no doubt. Women characterize this style of speech as men acting as if they know everything by speaking with such certainty. Often it results in shutting down women. Women are afraid to question or add their own take on an idea; that is, because of a man's certainty and unquestionable, authoritative style, a woman might hesitate to raise a doubt or an inquiry.

5. Women engage in rapport talk trying to "connect" with others.

   True. Women assume the social maintenance role in communication, and it is paramount that they build relationship with others through a rapport style of communication. Men engage in more report talk. "Just the facts" is a popular mantra when women describe men's speech style.

   Women assume a more relational approach and men assume more of a content approach to communication. The important thing to remember here is that women want to have dialogue just to reinforce the fact that the relationship exists and is important. The topic of the conversation is less important than the fact that a conversation is taking place. As communication experts Dana Ivy and Phil Backlund (2004) suggest: "No wonder men often think that women talk on and on about nothing. No wonder women often think men's relationships (and, sometimes, men themselves) are superficial. What's going on here? It's not that women are insecure chatterboxes who have nothing better to do than carry on long, pointless conversations because they need relational reinforcement. . . . What's going on here is that, in general, women and men use communication for different purposes and get their 'relational goodies' in dramatically different ways" (p. 197).

   Deborah Tannen (1994), a linguist who has extensively studied sex differences in speech style, describes a type of rapport talk women engage in as "troubles-talk." She cites an example of the ramifications and possible negative impact of troubles-talk: "Another woman told me that the troubles-talk impasse accounted for one source of frustration she experienced with her office-mate. . . . She would frequently initiate what she thought would be pleasant complaint-airing sessions, in which she'd talk about situations that bothered her just to talk about them, maybe in order to understand them better. But her office-mate would begin to tell her what she could do to improve the situation. This left her feeling condescended to and frustrated" (p. 71).

A possible hazard of women engaging in "troubles-talk" is that men interpret it literally. A woman may earn a reputation as a chronic complainer, or worse, a whiner, always talking and complaining about her problems. She risks being seen as unable to solve the problems that arise at work.

6. Men focus on "safe" topics, such as work and sports.

   True. The topics of conversation chosen by men tend to be "safe" topics, such as work, sports, and financial matters. Men's speech tends to revolve around external things and usually involves factual communication, not feelings or inner thoughts. In contrast, women will incorporate more person-centered topics and initiate interpersonal matters. Their speech is more apt to deal with feelings than men's topics of conversation do. As C. Brown and Nelson (2009) suggest, "Women talk about everything and anything. You name it. Women will reveal their insecurities, their latest diet, the trials of their uterus, their dreams and the list goes on. Any topic is fair game. Two women strangers sitting next to each other on a two-hour plane ride will arrive at their destination knowing how many children each has, their marital troubles, any school dilemmas, and what kind of birth control they each use" (p. 42).

   Psychologist Dr. Judith Tingley (1994) once described the differences in women's and men's conversation topics. It stemmed from a sailing lesson she took with four men and a male instructor. In Tingley's words, "The majority of the conversation centered on business and money. There was no discussion of people, feelings or relationships. No one mentioned a wife, a child, a brother or sister, a mother or father. The conversation was almost totally about each individual man and what he had done or seen or been, relative to sports, business or money. Men are private about anything having to do with relationships, feelings and emotions. They usually only disclose to significant others the private aspects of their lives" (p. 24).

7. Women are direct with requests.

    False. Women tend to beat around the bush when making requests. They will also lengthen the request as a softening mechanism to ease the force of an assertive act; that is, asking someone to do something needs to be balanced with deference. Often both men and women will complain they are not sure what a woman is asking or if she is even asking them to do something. It might sound like this: "Did you say you were headed to the copy room? Oh, never mind. I know you are busy with that deadline and have a lot going on," which is a disguise for the real request: "I need a copy of this contract." Women's requests can be so indirect that they don't sound like requests at all.

    Another strategy employed by women has been identified by speech communication professors Deborah Borisoff and Lisa Merrill (1992). It is the compound request, or "How many words shall I use to make my wishes known?" This lengthening of the request serves as a polite form of speech. Compare "Type this now" with "Will you type this now?" The person in the first example is issuing a command, and in the second example the person is still making a request but the addressee is free to refuse. Both strategies, direct and polite, are necessary skills in the workplace.

    Ask the group to respond to these questions in order to understand the complicated anatomy of a request:

1. Why doesn't she just say what she means?

2. Is her indirectness a form of insecurity?

3. What happens when a woman is direct in her request?

4. Are direct requests always preferable? In what situations?

8. Men apologize more than women.

   False. Women apologize more often than men. Women are frequently told to stop apologizing all the time. It is often perceived as eroding their credibility. Speech pathologist Lillian Glass (1993) claims that men "have more difficulty apologizing" and woman "can apologize more readily and easily." She suggests that men use less emotion when apologizing and women employ more emotion when they apologize (p. 59).

   Women tend to be indirect and lengthen
   their requests as a softening device.

   ---

9. Women incorporate more indirect verb forms (might, would, should, or could).

   True. Women employ more indirect verb forms in their speech. Indirect verb forms are sometimes perceived to weaken speech and make it less forceful or certain. Consider the following contrasts:

   He: We benefit from the extended deadline.

   She: We would benefit from the extended deadline.

   He: It is detrimental to our business.

   She: It might be detrimental to our business.

   He: I have a question.

   She: Could I ask a question?

Men use less emotion when apologizing.

---

10. Men are self-effacing in their speech.

   False. Women employ more self-effacing speech patterns. As discussed, women apologize more and employ more polite forms of speech, disclaimers, and softening strategies.

   C. Brown and Nelson (2009) cite examples from women participants in their training sessions:

   > Walk around your office listening to women talk. Does she sound soft spoken, self-effacing and compliant? Women have internalized this socially imposed stereotype. In many cases, women are reluctant to speak out and express themselves in public.

   > We see this with women at gender-communication seminars. They are paying to be there, and even after we call on them, they still ask our permission to speak.

   > It sounds a little something like this:

   > > I was wondering if I could ask you . . .

   > > May I ask you one thing?

   > > Could I ask a question?

   > > I would like to ask . . .

   > > Would it be all right if I ask you?

   > Others use apologetic sentence intros, as if the opinion that follows needs justification or a disclaimer:

   > > No offense, but . . .

   > > Not to sound mean, but . . .

   > > I'm not trying to stir up problems, but . . .

   > You rarely hear a man start a sentence by disclaiming or asking permission (p. 41).

Section 2: Different Speech Styles, Outcomes, and Missed Connections

Exercise 2.2. Case Study: A Comment Hiding in a Question

Goal

Identify how women present a comment embedded in a question.

Objectives

- Understand why women may employ indirect styles of communication.
- Analyze alternative ways in which women can make a comment.

Timing of Exercise

15–20 minutes total:

5–10 minutes to read the case and talk in small groups

10 minutes to hear responses from each group or from a sample of groups

Materials

Handout: Case Study: A Comment Hiding in a Question, chart paper and easel, markers

Slide 2.2

Setup

☐ Place the participants in coed groups of five to eight.

☐ Ask the participants to read the handout. The content for the handout includes the case study and questions.

☐ Ask each group to assign a scribe who will takes notes on the group's answers to the questions.

☐ Address each question with the entire class and ask for the individual group answers.

Slide 2.2

A Comment Hiding in a Question

Case Study: A Comment Hiding in a Question

Audrey was presenting a training session on strategies for handling bullies in the workplace. Here is the exchange that followed when she completed her list of tactics and strategies:

Audrey: Well, that concludes my suggestions for strategies you can employ for disarming the bully at work.

Female participant: Do you think that those are the only ways you can deal with a bully?

Audrey: Sounds like you have another idea on how to handle the office bully.

Female participant: Well, I was thinking of another strategy I have used.

Audrey: Would you like to share it with the class?

Female participant: Okay.

Questions

1. Did this exchange sound like a lot of work to get to the point of her sharing her idea?

2. What was the hidden comment in her question?

3. How would a male participant present the same idea?

Debrief

The contribution that the female participant was trying to make was an excellent illustration of women's indirect style of communication. At times, it can feel like you are playing twenty questions. Let's guess what she is really saying. So a question is not really a question; rather, it is a comment. "Are you going to do it like that?" is code for "I don't think you should do it like that."

> When a woman is placed in a position in which being assertive and forceful is necessary, she is faced with a paradox.

What is the underpinning to this indirect and often confusing style that women employ in their communication? Men and some women are frustrated by being on the receiving end of this confusion and will remark, "Just say it, woman!" But what happens to her when she is direct? She gets her hand slapped not only by men but also by other women. Her dilemma is the darned-if-I-do and darned-if-I-don't dilemma. A more direct approach would put her at risk of being labeled or called "pushy," "demanding," or "coming off too strong." Robin Lakoff (1990a), a professor of linguistics, offers an apt description of this double bind: "When a woman is placed in a position in which being assertive and forceful is necessary, she is faced with a paradox; she can be a good woman but bad executive or professional; or vice versa. To do both is impossible. As long as a woman stays in 'her place,' at home and in private, the contradiction does not surface" (p. 206). Phillips and Ferguson (2004) suggest, "Whenever a person behaves in a way that defies social expectations, anxiety increases. When men speak up, they are comfortable with the role of 'speaker,' though they may still have fears about public speaking. A woman speaker not only has to manage the psychological anxiety of public speaking that is common to both men and women, but has to manage the anxiety surrounding the role conflict as well. After all, if we're too feminine, how can we be leaders? If we are too masculine, we aren't 'normal' women" (p. 33).

training tip

A discussion that builds from Chapter One's discussion of an androgynous style would provide a solution to this dilemma. Also, emphasize that stepping outside the gender box is necessary sometimes for both men and women. Sometimes we have to take risks and question what is "normal."

Exercise 2.3. Case Study: Why Do I Have to Sugarcoat Everything for a Woman?

Goal

Identify how men present comments and feedback.

Objectives

- Understand why men may employ direct styles of communication.

- Explore alternative ways in which men can make a comment.

Timing of Exercise

15–20 minutes total:

5–10 minutes to read the case and talk in small groups

10 minutes to hear the responses from each group or a sample of groups

Materials

Handout: Case Study: Why Do I Have to Sugarcoat Everything for Women?, chart paper and easel, markers

Slide 2.3

Setup

☐ Place participants in coed groups of five to eight.

☐ Ask the participants to read the handout. The content for the handout includes the case study and questions.

☐ Ask each group to assign a scribe who will takes notes on the group's answers to the questions.

☐ Address each question with the entire class and ask for the individual group answers.

Slide 2.3

Why Do I Have to Sugarcoat Everything for Women?

Source: Copyright © 2012 by Audrey Nelson and Claire Damken Brown.

Case Study: Why Do I Have to Sugarcoat Everything for Women?

Jean: Bill, how do you think my presentation went for the management committee?

Bill: I have seen you do better. It wasn't your strongest presentation.

Source: Copyright © 2012 by Audrey Nelson and Claire Damken Brown.

Questions

1. How would you characterize Bill's communication style?

2. How do you think Jean felt when she received his feedback?

3. Would you change how Bill delivered his feedback to Jean? How?

Debrief

Men often claim that women ask trick questions. "She asked me, so I told her. And I told her the truth. Can't stand the heat, get out of the kitchen." No question about it, men have a more direct style of communication. On the receiving end, women accuse men of being inconsiderate, uncaring, and unfeeling. It is blunt force for women. From his perspective, he is simply answering the question. A man once said, "A woman at work told me I needed to go to charm school after I provided the evaluation and feedback she asked for. What a trap. She asked for it, but she couldn't take it! What's a guy to do?" The downside of the direct style is it does not take into consideration the receiver's feelings. In fact, the feedback may be lost to the receiver because she may be offended and hurt by the direct and sometimes confrontational style. Women often walk away from a meeting feeling as if they have just been hit with an emotional baseball bat.

> One advantage of men's direct style is that no one has to play twenty questions.

One advantage of men's direct style is that no one has to play twenty questions. You know where he stands, and he doesn't beat around the bush. He is right to the point. So it economizes on time. Additional differences in speech style and potential miscommunications are listed in slide 2.4.

Slide 2.4

GENDER GABBER DILEMMA: Process Versus Goal

Source: Copyright © 2012 by Audrey Nelson and Claire Damken Brown.

Women tend to be process-oriented and men are more goal-oriented in their speech styles. Ask a man what time it is, and he will simply provide the time. Ask a woman what time it is, and she will tell you how to build a clock. "Get to the point" and "What is the bottom line" were born from male culture. Women talking with other women will often forget what the point of the conversation was. Women's speech is rich with details, anecdotes, and information. The male is a man of few words. We know in the business world that everything runs fast and people are rewarded for multitasking and getting a lot done. Talking in one-sentence answers is rewarded and championed in male culture. However, as one woman engineer put it, "There are times when details are critical and necessary."

C. Brown and Nelson (2009) offer the *pyramid style* as a possible technique for women to employ when speaking to men:

> If you tend to be a ramblin' kind of woman, we recommend speaking in *pyramid style*. When a man asks a question, begin your answer with a one-word or one-sentence explanation. Imagine this as the top of the pyramid, the smallest part. Good. You've given him what he wants: direct and to the point. Now, if you must elaborate, shorten your descriptive explanation by half. Finish with silence. If he wants you to go on, he will ask for it. But most of the time, you won't hear him begging for more. He's too busy doing the internal happy dance that you cut to the chase. If he doesn't request more info, you're done. Turns out, he does not want to hear the history of everything you know about the topic. It may feel unfinished to you, but he is satisfied [p. 38].

Lakoff (1990a) coined the term *tag question*. A brief examination of the anatomy of a question is warranted by examining in slide 2.5 how a statement, question, and tag question compare.

Slide 2.5

TRICK QUESTIONS: Is It a Statement, Question, or Tag Question?

Statement: I need the report tomorrow.

Question: Will the report be ready tomorrow?

Tag question: I need the report tomorrow. Can you do it?

Source: Copyright © 2012 by Audrey Nelson and Claire Damken Brown.

training tip

Note that a tag question is often accompanied by a rise in pitch at the end of the question, completing the sentence. Emphasize that it is difficult to compartmentalize communication behavior into verbal and nonverbal. This is an excellent illustration of where verbal and nonverbal communication intersect and add meaning or confusion in the case of the tag question.

Lakoff (1994) suggests that asking questions shows women's insecurity and hesitancy in communication. Women's speech is said to be more polite and considerate—the tag question is a case in point. It does not force agreement but rather is solicitous and democratic. However, the tag question can become a sort of Pandora's box. Now she has opened up the potential for denial of the request.

Is there a place for the tag question? Yes, when a woman wants to hear another opinion or input. Are there situations when a tag question may be inappropriate? Yes, when there are no ifs, ands, or buts and something must get done, or if the woman has a strong opinion or perspective. For women, potentially the tag question can become a burden because it is vague. In the final evaluation, women should ask, "What is my goal?"

- Just say it; don't qualify it! Another technique employed by women more than men is the use of qualifiers. Here are some common qualifiers (in italics) used by women:

  Well, no.

  I was thinking, we could leave at 2 P.M.

  It's time to go, *I guess.*

  It seems to me that is a good idea.

  I wonder if we should pursue that contract.

  Employing qualifiers is a way that women counterbalance being direct. Again, this linguistic strategy could be argued to serve as a technique allowing for input and consideration of other ideas. However, if the woman feels definite and does not want to appear tentative on an issue, she should eliminate the qualifier.

Another technique employed by women more than men is the use of qualifiers.

- Let me introduce you to my disclaimer: the ultimate mitigation. Women often employ disclaimers in introductory remarks. Research has identified various types of disclaimers that serve different functions:

  1. Suspending judgment. Function: Ward off emotional judgment. "I don't want you to get angry, but . . ."

  2. Cognitive disclaimers. Function: Avoid disbelief or suspicions of poor judgment. "This may not make sense . . ."

3. Credentialing. Function: Identify special attributes of the speaker when the anticipated reaction may be negative. "Some of my closest contacts are Japanese, but . . ."

4. Hedging. Function: Speaker is not adamant about their point. "I could be wrong, but . . ." (Eakins & Eakins, 1978, p. 45).

One could argue that disclaimers could be viewed as verbal strategies to mitigate possible negative reactions to what a woman says. But the flip side of this strategy is that disclaimers can weaken women's speech. Why should a woman put herself down? When women need to take a firm stand, minimal or no use of disclaimers is advisable.

When women need to take a firm stand, minimal or no use of disclaimers is advisable.

According to Mindell (1995), "If the hedge adds no meaning, simply omit it." She also recommends that if real uncertainty forces a woman to hedge, she should use "strong hedges." Slide 2.6 shows some examples of alternatives to hedges.

Slide 2.6
Alternatives to Hedges

Hedge	Strong Alternative
I think it will be a good quarter.	It should be a good quarter.
I would like to . . .	I aim at . . .
I think this is about . . .	This is about . . .
The way I see it . . .	Apparently . . .

Source: Mindell, 1995, p. 56.

Exercise 2.4. Compare Most Direct to Least Direct: How Do I Ask the Question?

Goal

Create an awareness of the gender differences in how questions are asked.

Objectives

- Understand the pros and cons of lengthening a request.

- Explore alternative ways to ask a question.

Timing of Exercise

15–20 minutes total:

5–10 minutes to lengthen the question and talk in small groups

10 minutes to hear responses from each group or a sample of groups

Materials

Handout: Compare Most Direct to Least Direct: How Do I Ask the Question?, chart paper and easel, markers

Slide 2.7

Setup

☐ Place the participants in coed groups of five to eight.

☐ The content for the handout is the same as the content on slide 2.7. Distribute the handout.

☐ Ask the participants to start with the most-direct request: Get the report.

☐ Ask each group to assign a scribe who will takes notes on the group's diagram from most direct to least direct.

☐ Ask the scribe to write the group's diagram on flip-chart paper to allow the individual groups to share with the larger group.

☐ Address each question with the entire class and ask for the individual group answers.

Slide 2.7

COMPARE MOST DIRECT TO LEAST DIRECT:
How Do I Ask the Question?

Use more particles (will you, please, won't you), order the request differently, incorporate polite forms of speech (please), and make the question longer by the fifth example. With each step, the question gradually becomes more indirect.

Begin with:

1. Most direct . . . . Get the report.

2. Less direct . . . .

3. Less direct . . . .

4. Less direct . . . .

5. Least direct . . . .

Questions

1. How would you respond to the most-direct request?

2. How would you respond to the least-direct request?

3. Are there appropriate contexts where these two different styles (most direct and least direct) could be used at work? Name them. What kinds of situations?

Debrief

A useful polite strategy that women employ is the lengthening of requests. Women usually accomplish this with the incorporation of particles. The shorter the request, the more force it conveys. Inherent in the most-direct request is an implied threat for noncompliance, and it is usually reserved for speakers of superior status. Some might argue that when a woman lengthens the request, she weakens it. Compliance might become questionable. However, the more-direct style may be perceived as a command and met with resistance because it is perceived as less respectful.

An example of most direct, "Get me the report," gradually becomes less direct with length and politeness: "Will you get the report" or "Will you please get the report." Examples of an extreme compounding of indirectness and politeness might be, "It would be helpful, if you are not too busy and could spare the time, to get me the report."

training tip

This summary section emphasizes the importance of combining male and female linguistic strategies. That is, women and men can borrow from each other and combine linguistic choices with their own. This discussion can refer back to Chapter One and the value and merit of an androgynous and code-switching approach to speech communication.

The relationship between gender and language is complicated and complex. Men and women assume different roles, which are reflected in their linguistic choices. Despite these sex differences, communication can be satisfying and successful between men and women. The key is to develop a kind of gender cultural competence.

First it requires an understanding of the underpinnings—what drives the linguistic style—and then an androgynous or code-switching approach. Tannen (1990) believes that men and women "would do well to learn strategies more typically used by members of the other group—not to switch over entirely, but to have more strategies at their disposal" (p. 120). This combined understanding and expanding of one's linguistic behavioral repertoire is fundamental to enhancing speech communication between men and women. Men and women can learn new strategies from each other.

Use the Action Steps slides (on pages 62 and 63) for men and women as part of your summary for the material you presented from this chapter.

Slide 2.8
Action Steps for Men

- Acknowledge that women's more polite style of speech does not imply that they are uninformed or weak.

- Acknowledge that other styles (indirect and polite) have uses in business contexts.

- Incorporate less of a command style of speech with women, especially when making requests.

- Encourage women to initiate topics.

- Offer both an empathetic and constructive response when providing feedback.

- Acknowledge that women build rapport and may do this through "troubles-talk."

- Realize that when women ask a question, it may be a tactic for offering a comment or opinion.

- Request a short answer from women.

- Encourage women to be assertive in their speech.

Source: Copyright © 2012 by Audrey Nelson and Claire Damken Brown.

Slide 2.9

Action Steps for Women

- Realize that men are task-oriented in their speech and don't be offended if they omit any rapport communication.

- Incorporate more one-sentence answers and report only necessary information and facts.

- Express solutions with your problems and cue men when you are venting.

- Monitor speech styles that may appear tentative and cast doubt on your conviction (for example, hedging, tag questions, qualifiers, and disclaimers).

- Make direct requests.

- Provide feedback that doesn't get lost in the overuse of tentative speech strategies.

- Monitor apologies, especially their frequency.

Source: Copyright © 2012 by Audrey Nelson and Claire Damken Brown.

CHAPTER 3

Gender Conversation Technicalities

Interruptions, Overlapping, and Other Turn-Taking Dilemmas

> *We take the view that the use of interruptions by males is a display of dominance or control to the female (and to any witnesses), just as the parent's interruption communicates an aspect of parental control to the child and to others present.*
>
> —Candace West and Don Zimmerman
> (1998, p. 172)

Learning Objectives

- Examine talk patterns, such as the impact of interruptions when men and women interact.

- Explore the concept of turn taking, in terms of the communication process and how women and men talk.

- Identify the overlapping process.

- Understand men's self-directed and women's other-oriented communication styles.

- Suggest action steps for men and women to improve their communication skills to be strategic about talk patterns, such as interruptions and turn taking.

Introduction

Communication patterns have been studied that reveal the technical aspects of how men and women talk to each other. These talking patterns indicate how the conversation is managed between two or more communicators. Patterns illustrate whose turn it is to speak or turn taking, who gets interrupted, and how interruptions happen, including a type of interruption called *overlapping*. Talking patterns indicate that men in general are self-directed in their communication style while women are other-directed or other-oriented. The men's focus is internal, mentioning "me or I" more often than women; women's focus is external, mentioning "we or you" more often in conversations than men.

Overall these patterns of interruptions and overlapping are related to dominance of the conversation. One person interrupting another is making an effort to take the floor away from the speaker. This is often viewed as disruptive behavior and not an appropriate sequential turn-taking pattern. The interrupter is taking power away from the speaker by taking control of the conversation. The person who has the floor or the group's attention is viewed as the one with the power. Someone who overlaps the speaker is talking at the same time as the speaker. It also can be viewed as an attempt to demonstrate power by expressing one's views while the speaker is still talking, resulting in taking the focus away from the speaker. Add to this the gender of the speaker and more patterns are revealed.

Timing for Unit

1 hour to 1 hour and 15 minutes

Materials for Unit

Handouts, chart paper and easel, markers

Slides 3.1 through 3.4

Section 1: How He and She Interrupt and Overlap Their Talk

The talking patterns between two speakers are recognized as turn taking: one person stops and another person starts. In 1974, a model of conversational turn taking was developed by Sacks, Schegloff, and Jefferson (as cited in West & Zimmerman, 1998) that provided "a systematic approach to speaker alternation in naturally occurring conversation" (p. 166). The model expects one person to talk at a time and that changing speakers keeps occurring. When a person has a turn to talk, it means that she or he has "the right and obligation to speak" until a transition point occurs, such as the end of a sentence or specifically identifying the next speaker (pp. 166–167). In general, men speak longer and take more turns than women do in mixed-sex groups.

In general men speak longer and take more turns
than women do in mixed-sex groups.

An interruption occurs when the second speaker does not allow the first speaker to reach the transition point. The interrupter "breaks in and starts talking, causing the other to stop before finishing her [or his] train of thought" (C. Brown & Nelson, 2009, p. 68). An overlap is a "brief stretch of simultaneous speech initiated by a 'next' speaker just before the current speaker arrives at a possible transition place" (Zimmerman & West, 1975, cited in West & Zimmerman, 1998, p. 167).

training tip

This chapter builds on past discussions that examined how men and women speak to each other. This chapter works best when combined with other chapters, especially Chapter Two, "He Speaks, She Speaks: What Different Things They Say," or Chapter Six, "Men, Women, and Conflict." Use discussions from earlier parts of the program or seminar, such as Chapter Two, to continue to look at men's and women's speaking patterns.

His and Hers: Turn Taking, Interruptions, and Overlapping Talk

Much research demonstrates that men interrupt women more than women interrupt men and that this interruption is an indicator of power and dominance (West, 1998, p. 397). Linguist Deborah Tannen describes a review of research where there was not a constant pattern of men interrupting women (Tannen, 1994, p. 232). While that behavior did happen, the review also found that in same-sex groups, women interrupted women more than men interrupted men. Other research has shown that in same-sex groups, women and men interrupt at the same rate. There is a difference in the type of interruptions; some interrupters were disruptive and changed the topic while others showed enthusiasm and support for the speaker. Speakers who were excited and enthusiastic talked over others and were referred to as "overlapping" (p. 233). Positive overlaps included verbalizations such as, "Uh-huh," "I agree," "Yeah," "That's right," or "Interesting." Women use these phrases that acknowledge the speaker and show they are listening more frequently than men.

> Women use positive interruptions or overlaps
> such as "I agree," "Uh-huh," or "That's right,"
> to acknowledge the speaker and indicate they
> are listening.

Speech communication professors Deborah Borisoff and Lisa Merrill looked at research on families and "found that fathers were more likely to interrupt children than were mothers, and both parents were more likely to interrupt girls than boys" (1992, p. 36). "Some researchers found women were more frequently interrupted than were men, regardless of whether women or men were doing the interrupting" (p. 36). Studies indicated that those with more power interrupted others more often than those with less power and those with less power were interrupted more often (p. 37). Julia Wood, professor of humanities, reviewed the research and determined "that men are more likely to interrupt to control conversation by challenging other speakers or wresting the talk stage from them, whereas women interrupt to indicate interest and respond to others" (2005, p. 122). An interesting perspective from Wood (1998) suggests that men's banter behavior has them interrupting more than women since their interruptions are viewed as "normal and good-natured" behavior expected within male conversation (as cited in Wood, 2005, p. 122). Women may view abrupt interruptions that change the topic as rude and impolite in terms of their relationship-oriented socialization.

> Women interrupt to show interest and support for the speaker more often than men.

Women being interrupted more often than men may have an impact on women's careers. By not having the opportunity to complete their ideas and contribute on an equal footing in group settings, women may be viewed as less assertive, not having valuable ideas, not able to contribute to the group, or not confident in expressing their ideas. These perspectives lower the likelihood that a woman will be seen as having leadership qualities and ultimately affect her career advancement. To ensure that a woman takes back control when interrupted, here are some phrases she may use: "Just a second . . . ," "I'm not quite done yet," "Hold on, I'll be with you in a moment," "Let's hold questions until I'm finished," "Thanks for that insight; I'll finish now," or "Hold that thought" (C. Brown & Nelson, 2009, pp. 75–76). Brown and Nelson suggest that if interrupted, a woman can gain control by making brief eye contact with the interrupter (not staring or "shooting daggers"); she can simply establish eye contact and make a statement, using the person's name if she knows it: "Bryan, I'll take comments in a moment." Then she can make eye contact with the group and finish her thoughts (p. 74). She may also "lean forward" toward the interrupter, speak louder, or stand up if seated to get the focus back on her (p. 75). Certainly men may use these techniques, too, to gain the floor back. However, given women's often-lower status, it's imperative that she use these behaviors to be seen and heard.

Exercise 3.1. "It's Not Polite to Interrupt!"

Goal

Begin a conversation about how women and men interrupt each other.

Objectives

- Get the groups talking about the impact of men's and women's interruption behaviors in the workplace.

- Identify gender differences in interruptions and look at their relationship to power and status.

Timing of Exercise

20 minutes

Materials

5 index cards prepared for volunteers, chart paper and easel, markers

Slide 3.1

Setup

- [ ] Use this exercise to get the participants thinking about their perceptions of how and why men and women interrupt each other.

- [ ] Conduct the exercise in front of the class with four or five volunteers and then process it with the entire group.

- [ ] Prior to the exercise, prepare five index cards with the following information for each volunteer's role:

  1. Interrupt: Interrupt the person talking as often as possible.

  2. Overlap: Overlap the person talking. While the person is still talking, you start talking. Continue to overlap the person talking as often as possible.

  3. Turn taking: Wait until the person has finished talking, then it's your turn to talk.

  4. Normal talker: Talk as you normally would about the selected topic of conversation.

  5. If you have five volunteers, prepare an extra Interrupt card for the fifth volunteer.

- [ ] Select four or five volunteers from the participants. Have them join you in front of the training room.

- [ ] Hand each volunteer an index card with instructions for the role each one will play during the discussion.

- [ ] Select a central theme for the discussion by the volunteers. For example, ask the volunteers or the audience for the general topic for discussion. Topics might be the importance of voting, maintaining one's health, the need for a career plan, and so on.

- [ ] Tell the group of volunteers to start the conversation on the selected topic. Remind the volunteers to follow the instructions on their index cards during the discussion. Have the volunteers talk for about four or five minutes or long enough for the participants to determine the volunteers' different roles.

☐ Stop the conversation at four or five minutes.

☐ Ask the larger group of participants what they observed about the conversation.

☐ Ask the volunteers for comments on what they observed and how they felt when trying to communicate during the discussion.

☐ Ask the volunteers and the larger group of participants if they observed any behaviors they thought were gender specific.

Slide 3.1

Interruption Behaviors

Talking Patterns

Turn Taking

Interrupting

Overlapping

Source: Copyright © 2012 by Audrey Nelson and Claire Damken Brown.

Debrief

The volunteers and the larger group of participants will note the different roles of the speakers: someone talking normally, someone interrupting others, and someone waiting their turn to speak. The difference between interrupting and overlapping a speaker may not be clear to the participants; the participants and volunteers may consider overlapping as another person interrupting others. Use this as an opportunity to discuss the differences between turn taking, disruptive and cooperative interruptions, and overlapping.

Write the participants' comments on the chart paper for future reference during the session. In order not to forget particular comments or questions, the facilitator may record them on chart paper and address them later in the program.

Exercise 3.2. Case Study: When He Interrupts Her

Goal

Identify the impact of men's and women's interruption behaviors.

Objectives

- Explore the men's and women's expectations for turn taking and managing interruptions.

- Suggest what behaviors could have been done differently to improve communication between Juanita and Harry.

Timing of Exercise

20 minutes total:

5 minutes to read the case and talk in small groups

15 minutes to hear the responses from each group or a sample of the groups

Materials

Handout: Case Study: "Let Me Finish!," chart paper and easel, markers

Optional: Create a slide to display the case study.

Setup

☐ Place the participants in coed groups of five to eight.

☐ The content for the handout includes the case study and questions. Distribute the handout and ask the participants to read it.

☐ Ask each group to assign a scribe who will takes notes on the group's answers to the case study questions.

☐ Address each question with the entire class and ask for the individual group answers.

Case Study: "Let Me Finish!"

The group meeting started ten minutes ago. Juanita was prepared to give her short report when her turn came. Her supervisor, Sheree, usually went around the room to hear updates from each team member. It was now Juanita's turn.

Juanita began, "This segment of the software testing found several errors that . . ." Harry jumped in, "There's nothing wrong with that software. In fact, you were testing the wrong version. Now would be a good time to discuss how to access the latest version of the software. I have instructions to share with the group."

Juanita glared at Harry. "Let me finish!" she said loudly. "No manners," she mumbled, barely audible under her breath.

Harry, startled at Juanita's uncharacteristic bossiness, replied sternly, "You are finished. You were finished as soon as you accessed the wrong software. And not only that, you . . ."

"Okay, kids, that's enough," broke in Sheree. "Let's have Juanita finish her update, and then I want to hear about the software versions from Harry."

Source: Copyright © 2012 by Audrey Nelson and Claire Damken Brown.

Questions

1. What happened?

2. List Juanita's and Harry's behaviors that helped and that hurt the discussion.

3. List Sheree's behaviors that helped and that hurt the discussion.

4. Was gender a concern in this communication? How?

5. How would you have managed the discussion?

6. What could both parties do to improve the situation?

Debrief

As supervisor, Sheree appears to be in charge of the group meeting. She has set up a turn-taking process that seems to have worked in the past since she continues to use it. One team member finishes an update, and then the next team member continues. The floor belongs to Juanita when Harry interrupts and takes the floor away from her. This is an example of a disruptive interruption; he takes the floor while she is still talking and changes the subject to one he wants for continuing the discussion.

Juanita waits for Harry's sentence to end and then she speaks. In addition to the phrase, "Let me finish," Juanita could use any of the phrases mentioned earlier in this chapter to regain the floor. She attempts to gain the floor back by using eye contact and a loud voice to call the group's attention back to herself. Using brief eye contact and looking at the interrupter (Harry) is appropriate; glaring at the interrupter is not appropriate because it appears as a challenge (see the following chapter entitled, "Women, Men, and Unspoken Messages"). Speaking a bit louder when attempting to gain the floor back is a good technique to use; it calls attention back to the original speaker. However, in this case Harry views Juanita's glaring and loud voice as a challenge. Harry accepts the challenge and interrupts and counters Juanita with his own stern voice. A man's voice tends to have a deeper pitch; add to this Harry's stern speaking style and it appears that he is challenging her back.

Sheree uses a cooperative interruption, an interruption that attempts to guide the conversation and set a positive tone, although her use of "Okay, kids, that's enough" appears to be sarcastic, as if she's treating them like children. She could use a more positive statement. A better statement for Sheree would be, "Okay, people, let's stay on track. Let's have Juanita finish . . ." and so on.

Was gender a factor in this communication exchange? No. Try reversing Juanita's and Harry's roles and changing Sheree to Charlie. The issue of gender in this case is that most research indicates that men make more interruptions than women and that women are interrupted more often by men than by women in mixed-sex groups. Having this knowledge, Juanita could prepare ahead of time by knowing how to manage interruptions, how to gain the floor back, and how she may partner with other team members to support her views at the meeting. Likewise, knowing that men tend to make the most interruptions, Harry can work on not interrupting others at the group meetings, letting each person have his or her turn, and sharing his views and information where and when appropriate at the meeting.

Section 2: Women's and Men's Perspectives: Other and Self

Exercise 3.3. "Me, Me, Me, Me or You, You, You, You?"

Goal

Understand the self-directed perspective versus the other-oriented perspective.

Objectives

- Get the groups talking about the impact of men's self-directed orientation and women's other-directed orientation.

- Identify and discuss gender differences in these styles and explore their relationship to power and status.

Timing of Exercise

20 minutes

Materials

Chart paper and easel, markers

Slide 3.2

Setup

☐ Use this exercise to get the participants thinking about their perceptions of the focus (internal or external) of men's and women's conversations.

☐ Conduct the exercise in dyads and then process it with the entire group.

☐ Ask the participants to stand and select partners, preferably someone they do not know. Note that some dyads will be same-sex and others will be mixed-sex.

☐ Ask the participants to identify the topic of the discussion. It could be news, TV, politics, favorite foods, how to be good parents, or another general topic. The facilitator may write a few of these topics on the flip chart and then ask for a quick show of hands on which topic is preferred. Select a topic that may provide discussion yet not be too adversarial, such as abortion rights or the right to prayer in the workplace. Tell the group the selected topic for discussion.

☐ Have the participants decide who is partner A and who is partner B. Note that the group will have a mixture of men and women as partners.

☐ Ask all those who are partner A to leave the training room and step into the hallway (or other private space where they are unable to hear the discussion in the main training room). Note that this exercise works best with up to fifty people. Beyond that, it may take too much time to have all partner A participants leave the room and return.

☐ Tell the partner B participants to remain in the room.

☐ Give the following instructions to the partner B participants:

1. At the signal to begin, partner B will start a conversation on the selected topic and keep the topic of conversation on partner A. For example, if the topic is the best restaurant in town, ask partner A: "What type of food do you like?" "Where do you like

to go out to eat?" "Do you do much cooking?" "Where would you take friends who were visiting to dinner?" or "Tell me about the best meal you had in a restaurant."

2. Partner B is to keep the conversation on partner A. Keep directing the conversation back to partner A's views and opinions on the selected topic.

☐ Tell the entire group of partner A participants to come back into the main training room and stand with their B partners.

☐ Remind the groups of the selected topic. Tell them they will have approximately five minutes to discuss the topic. At the signal to "go," partner B will begin the discussion.

☐ After five minutes stop the discussion.

☐ Ask the partner A participants who are women what the conversation was like for them. Select a few women partner A participants and hear their views. Then ask partner A participants who are men the same question. Hear from a few partner A men.

☐ Ask partner B participants what the conversation was like from their perspective. Ask both women and men partner B participants.

☐ Tell the participants they may sit down at their seats.

Slide 3.2

Internal and External Focus

Men: Self-directed

Women: Other-oriented

Source: Copyright © 2012 by Audrey Nelson and Claire Damken Brown.

Debrief

The purpose of this exercise is to get men and women thinking about their talk patterns. Men tend to be self-directed. This means they prefer to talk about themselves: what they are doing, what they think, what they know, or what they believe. The conversation is about them. This is not in a narcissistic sense; but because of their competitive socialization, they want to place themselves in a winning position. If they see that they may be losing, they ramp up and readily talk about why they should win, be the winner, and are better than others. Men are comfortable talking about themselves and their accomplishments. Even if one man does not have the same impressive background as the next man, he easily tends to exaggerate and inflate his good deeds or impressive work so that he is seen as a winner. Being a "winner" translates into being the leader, the most sought after, and the guy with the great reputation. Being self-directed is part of men's "outdo you" or "one-upping" communication behaviors. For example, Fred says his sales are the highest in the office. Then Jim says his sales are the highest in the region. Fred replies that he made more than $50,000 in commissions last year. Jim then states he made $50,000 in commissions last quarter.

> Men tend to be self-directed, thinking about their communication and the impact it has on them and not on others. This is not good or bad. It's simply a different way of evaluating one's own behaviors and situation.

A man tends to be self-directed, thinking about his communication and the impact it has on him and not on others. This is not good or bad. It's simply a different way of evaluating one's own behaviors and situation. When listening to others, a man tends to do the same thing: evaluate the words he hears in terms of how they affect him and his decisions. This is not indicative of a negative trait that men are self-centered or egotistical. It means that men tend to interpret what they hear and say in terms of the impact on themselves. This is helpful to men because they see themselves as competing with others (men and women) in the office. Men often perceive their own banter and talk as a game, and they are there to compete and be seen as winners. A high-power, high-status person has learned the competitive style and the importance of being self-directed in their communication style.

Women tend to be other-oriented. Women's talk patterns are aimed at the other person: their feelings, their thoughts, their desires, or what they'd like to do. The focus of the conversation is on the other person. This is because of the way women are socialized. Women learn to be relationship-oriented, and part of that socialization is a focus on ensuring that the relationship develops and carries forward. Women learn to put others' needs before their own needs. In many ways, women learn to care for the other person just as they care for the relationship. In the workplace, a woman's other orientation may be viewed as being a team player, concerned about her team members. However, because of this other orientation, a woman also may appear as not focused on her own skills and accomplishments; some may think she lacks confidence in herself to the detriment of her career success. "Toot your own horn" is a phrase often recommended to women as a reminder to speak up and let others know about their accomplishments and successes.

> Women tend to be other-oriented. Women's talk patterns are aimed at the other person: their feelings, their thoughts, their desires, or what they'd like to do. The focus of the conversation is on the other person.

Women talk and listen using the other orientation. Women listen for the other person's feelings and thoughts and tend to interpret them in terms of the relationship. Women speak using the tag questions and disclaimers mentioned in the previous chapter, softening their requests or comments in order to keep a level of politeness to maintain the relationship. She does not use her conversation to compete; she uses her conversation to understand others, gain acceptance, and build relationships. These are examples of the other-oriented communication style.

In this exercise the woman who is partner B, asking the questions, will usually find it "normal" to keep the conversation focused on the other person. The man who has the role of partner A, answering the questions about himself, will usually say it was "normal" since it was the same self-directed behavior to which he's accustomed. The roles that tend to take more effort are when the woman acts as partner A talking about herself—she will usually want to redirect the conversation back to be about the other person—and the man acts as partner B, asking questions and keeping the conversation focused on the other person. He may tend to want to add comments about his own experience.

Exercise 3.4. You, Me, and Chit-Chat at Work

Goal

Understand the self-directed perspective versus the other-oriented perspective.

Objectives

- Review men's self-directed orientation and women's other-directed orientation.

- Experience and discuss the gender differences in self-directed and other-directed orientations.

Timing of Exercise

20 minutes

Materials

Chart paper and easel, markers

Setup

☐ Use this exercise to get the participants thinking about their perceptions of the focus (internal or external) of men's and women's conversations.

☐ Conduct the exercise in dyads and then process it with the entire group.

☐ Ask the participants to stand and select a partner, preferably someone they do not know. Note that some dyads will be same-sex and others will be mixed-sex.

☐ Have the participants decide who is partner A and who is partner B. Note that the group will have a mixture of men and women as partners A and B.

☐ Ask all those who are partner A to leave the training room and step into the hallway (or other private space where they are unable to hear the discussion in the main training room). Note that this exercise works best with up to fifty people. Beyond that, it may take too much time to have all partner A participants leave the room and return.

☐ Tell partner B participants to remain in room.

☐ Give the following instructions to the partner B participants in the room:

　　1. At the signal to begin, partner B will start a "chit-chat" conversation with partner A. For example, partner B could ask partner A, "Where are you from?" "How long have you lived here?" "Do you have any brothers or sisters?" "Do you have a significant other?" or "Tell me about your family."

　　2. As soon as partner A asks a question about partner B (family, where from, and so on), partner B will stop the conversation and raise her or his hand.

☐ Tell the entire group of partner A participants to come back into the main training room and stand with their partners.

☐ Tell them they will have approximately three minutes for a discussion. At the signal to "go," partner B will start the discussion.

☐ Watch the discussion and the hands being raised by the partner B participants.

☐ Stop the exercise at three minutes whether or not all dyads have stopped talking. Partner B participants may lower their hands.

☐ Ask the partner B participants how long it took for their partner to flip the conversation back to them.

☐ Ask to see the hands of any remaining dyads that were still talking at the end of the three minutes. Check the composition of the dyads: were they same-sex women, men, or mixed-sex dyads? If they were mixed-sex dyads, who was partner B (asking the questions)—was it a man or woman?

☐ Tell the participants they may sit down at their seats.

Debrief

Women with their other orientation are good at gathering information that contributes to building a relationship. Although this exercise involves "chit-chat," the information gathered is valuable toward building a relationship and team. Women's chit-chat tends to be devalued as gossip or nonessential dialogue that interferes with getting the job done. However, chit-chat can be viewed as important to learning about individuals and building office camaraderie.

With this exercise, it is expected that the women who are partner A participants will quickly flip the conversation back to partner B, asking partner B a similar personal question about that person's hometown or family status. It is expected that when partner A is a man, it will take longer for him to flip the conversation back to partner B. The male same-sex dyad usually takes the longest time or may go the full three minutes without having partner A switch the conversation back to partner B. Men tend to be self-directed, so as partner A participants, they would be comfortable answering questions and discussing themselves. In terms of how quickly the dyads flip the conversation, it usually plays out in the following order: women same-sex dyads; mixed-sex dyads where partner B is a man and partner A is a woman; mixed-sex dyads where partner B is a woman and partner A is a man; and last, men same-sex dyads.

Use the Action Steps slides for men and women as part of your summary for the material you presented from this chapter.

Slide 3.3

Action Steps for Men

- Do not interrupt.

- Listen to the other's complete thought.

- Use the words *we* or *you* more often. Monitor how frequently you're using *I*.

- Make sure each person in the group has a turn to speak.

- Incorporate nonfluencies such as "Uh-huh," "Gee," and one- or two-word responses, such as "I agree," "Yeah," or "That works."

Source: Copyright © 2012 by Audrey Nelson and Claire Damken Brown.

Slide 3.4

Action Steps for Women

- Monitor how often you are interrupted or overlapped.

- Be prepared to be interrupted by knowing how to take the floor back.

- Use brief eye contact with the interrupter to signal that you're ready to take the floor back.

- Use suggested phrases to alert the interrupter that you will be finishing your statements.

   "Just a second," "I'm not quite done yet," "Hold on; I'll be with you in a moment," "Let's hold questions until I'm finished," "Thanks for that insight; I'll finish now," or "Hold that thought."

- Make sure that at group meetings you take the opportunity to speak and share your ideas with the group.

- Speak up about your accomplishments; use *I* more often.

Source: Copyright © 2012 by Audrey Nelson and Claire Damken Brown.

CHAPTER **4**

Women, Men, and Unspoken Messages

The combination of infants' biological differences and the responses
these invoke in caretakers establish very early that sex differences in
nonverbal behavior are expected and perceived.

—*Clara Mayo and Nancy M. Henley (1981, p. 6)*

Learning Objectives

- Understand differences in women's and men's nonverbal behaviors.

- Explore how facial expressions, touch, personal space, and vocal tones influence messages from men and women.

- Develop an awareness of first impressions and unspoken messages.

- Suggest action steps for men and women to improve knowledge and the use of nonverbal behaviors when communicating.

Introduction

We send verbal and nonverbal messages. Verbal messages constitute the words. Nonverbal messages are composed of all else, from facial expression to body movement to vocal sounds—not words—such as grunting or sighing. "Nonverbal communication is all elements of communication other than the words themselves. It includes not only gestures and movement, but also inflection, volume, and environmental factors such as space and color" (Wood, 2005, p. 129). While awake we are communicating all the time to those around us by what we say or don't say. Whether smiling, frowning, winking, or sighing, a person is sending a message to those around her or him. Just as men and women are socialized and learn to express themselves verbally in a style that suits their gender, they also learn nonverbal gender-appropriate ways to express themselves. In addition to socialization, an individual's culture also influences verbal and nonverbal behaviors and what may be viewed as appropriate communication behaviors for men and women.

Timing for Unit

2 hours and 45 minutes

Materials for Unit

Handouts, chart paper and easel, markers

Slides 4.1 through 4.11

Section 1: Unspoken Gender Messages

Exercise 4.1. Find Meaning in What You Don't Say

Goal

Start talking about men's and women's nonverbal behaviors in the workplace.

Objectives

- Define nonverbal communication.

- Begin to identify gender differences in nonverbal behavior.

Timing of Exercise

20 minutes

Materials

Handout: Find Meaning in What You Don't Say, chart paper and easel, markers

Slides 4.1 and 4.2

Setup

☐ Use this exercise as a warm-up to get the participants thinking about their ideas on nonverbal communication and how men and women communicate nonverbally.

☐ Conduct the exercise in dyads and process it with the entire group, or conduct it in groups of five to eight members, where each member shares his or her response, and then process it with the entire group.

☐ Ask the group to identify one person to be the scribe and another person to report on the group's discussion.

☐ Distribute the handout.

☐ When the facilitator starts discussing question number three on the handout, then display slide 4. 2 for example responses.

Slide 4.1
Nonverbal Communication

Kinesics: body movement, gestures

Haptics: touch, how and when people touch

Paralinguistics: vocal cues such as pitch, loudness, and
inflection patterns

Proxemics: personal space and distance

Artifacts: clothing, color, objects, jewelry, hairstyles, piercings

Source: Copyright © 2012 by Audrey Nelson and Claire Damken Brown.

Sample Handout Text: Find Meaning in What You Don't Say

Think about your behavior at work.

1. Can you not *not* communicate? How?

2. How would you define nonverbal communication?

3. List as many types of nonverbal behaviors as you can.

4. Identify which nonverbal behaviors you think are more
   characteristic of men versus women. Give reasons and examples.

Debrief

Nonverbal communication is everything except the written and
spoken word. People are always communicating; even silence sends a
message to those around you. Albert Mehrabian (1981), a professor at
the University of California, Los Angeles, found that when there were
conflicting verbal and nonverbal messages being sent, 55 percent of
the message's meaning came from facial expressions and body
movement; 38 percent came from vocal cues such as pitch, pauses, and
tone; and only 7 percent of the message's meaning came from the

spoken word. This means that over 90 percent of the meaning stems from nonverbal behaviors. "Nonverbal communication . . . includes body language (kinesics), vocal cues (paralinguistics), the use of space and distance (proxemics), touch (haptics), color, clothing, and artifacts" (Gamble & Gamble, 2003, p. 88).

Slide 4.2
Elements of Nonverbal Communication

Nonverbal communication includes but is not limited to the following:

- Touch
- Eye contact: gaze, glance, stare
- Volume, pitch, loudness of voice
- Use of personal space
- Gestures
- Facial expressions
- Pauses, silence
- Intonation, speaking pace
- Dress and general appearance
- Posture
- Smell
- Nonfluencies or vocal sounds: um, er, uh
- Vocal "fillers": you know, whatever, yeah

Source: Copyright © 2012 by Audrey Nelson and Claire Damken Brown.

Women and men tend to use nonverbal behaviors differently. For example, women tend to be more expressive when communicating; they use more facial expressions and gestures than men. Women smile more often than men. Women smile so often that it can be hard to know when the smile has a meaning of happiness (the situation deserves a smile), or the smile means embarrassed, angry, sad, forgetful, and so on. Men tend to smile only when they are happy or have heard something funny. Contrary to women, men's smiles are usually congruent with their feelings of happiness. Because men in general do not smile as often as women and are not as expressive in their gestures and facial expressions, some women (and even a few men who are expressive or emotionally demonstrable) may view men as emotionless or label them as cold and uncaring. Women who do not smile and look directly at the speaker may be viewed as upset, angry, unsupportive, or snobbish. Men who smile a lot (more than when they are happy) and stare at the speaker may be perceived as suspicious persons or troublemakers (Wood, 2005, p. 131). As the facilitator, relate the participants' comments and examples to earlier chapters on socialization and how they have learned gender-appropriate nonverbal behaviors.

> Women are more intuitive than men because they
> hear the verbal and see the nonverbal messages.

Women are more skilled than men at deciphering nonverbal messages (Nelson, 2004, p. 24). The generalization that women are more intuitive than men may relate to women's hearing the verbal and seeing the nonverbal messages. Women interpret both message channels, verbal and nonverbal, when assigning meaning to the message as a whole. Men tend to focus on the words or the content only of the messages they hear. Some of the reasoning for this is that those with lower status generally have to be adept at reading messages from every channel to ensure that they get the full message. When a person has low status, he or she wants to get as much information as possible from the high-status person in order to respond to them appropriately. In U.S. culture, people of high status, usually men or white people, do not need to pay attention to all message channels from a subordinate or lower-status person; it's enough for them to hear the words as the sole message. The group that has the power does not need to be skilled at reading or decoding the nonverbal messages of those with less power. However, for those with less power, reading nonverbal cues increases their survival and ability to succeed (Wood, 2005, p. 132). Women are more clued in than men to people's nonverbal gestures and feelings, and women use those messages to interpret the message as a whole.

Sample Handout Text: The Impact of Double Messages

Exercise 4.2. Double Messages

Goal

Understand the impact of double messages.

Objectives

- Explore double messages and their connection to nonverbal communication.

- Be aware of gender and double messages.

Timing of Exercise

15 minutes

Materials

Handout: The Impact of Double Messages, chart paper and easel, markers

Slide 4.3

Setup

☐ Either conduct this exercise in dyads and process it with the entire group, or conduct it in groups of five to eight members, where each member shares his or her response, and then process it with the entire group.

☐ Distribute the handout.

Slide 4.3

Double Messages

Double messages: when the verbal and nonverbal messages contradict

Mixed messages

Source: Copyright © 2012 by Audrey Nelson and Claire Damken Brown.

---

1. What happens when verbal and nonverbal messages contradict each other?

2. Do you believe the verbal or nonverbal message? Why? Share an example.

3. What is the impact in the workplace?

4. How do double messages affect men and women?

5. How do double messages affect your credibility and the credibility of others? Why?

Debrief

We use the term *double message* to refer to an individual's message in which the verbal and nonverbal meanings contradict each other. Based on research in the communication field, women seem to send more double messages than men. The incongruence in the messages sent generally affects women by lowering their perceived credibility. When the boss yells at his subordinate, Lakeysha, and she smiles back, what is the message she's sending? It's a mixed message. When Mary says his joke was awful but laughs anyway, what does she really mean? Was the joke bad or good? If a woman expresses her disappointment to her male colleague when he says it's his fault the project is delayed for two weeks, and then she smiles at him, what is he to understand? He may think, "Maybe the job delay isn't that bad after all." More times than not the man may walk away thinking the woman doesn't know what she wants or what to do next, thus lowering her credibility in his eyes.

Saving face may be a reason for some of women's double messages. For example, if a woman is in an embarrassing situation, she may smile as if to say she's all right even though she's upset with what just happened. If she expresses her anger at her employee, she may want to alleviate the other person's embarrassment or discomfort and smile as if to say, "I know you can do better." She may be using her smile to soften the blow or the severity of her words. Instead it negates the seriousness of her message and affects her work image. "Betty's so happy. She smiles all the time. She never gets mad at anyone." But can happy Betty be strict and stern, managing a team to meet a critical deadline? Men and women may want to be more conscious of their nonverbal messages and work to keep their verbal and nonverbal messages congruent.

Exercise 4.3. Behaviors That Are "On" or "Off" the Record

Goal

Establish the impact of nonverbal behaviors on men's and women's communication styles.

Objectives

- Define "on the record" in terms of nonverbal behaviors.

- Define "off the record" in terms of nonverbal behaviors.

- Understand how nonverbal behaviors are a critical component of women's and men's communication.

Timing of Exercise

15 minutes

Materials

Chart paper and easel, markers

Slide 4.4

Setup

☐ Display the slide, which has three true or false statements.

☐ Tell the group they have five minutes to talk with their immediate neighbors and decide if the questions are true or false.

☐ Ask the participants to define subtle nonverbal behaviors.

☐ Ask the participants to identify the distinction between off the record and on the record.

☐ At the end of five minutes, reconvene the groups and ask for their comments.

Slide 4.4

Behaviors That Are "On" or "Off" the Record

True or False?

1. Subtle nonverbal behaviors are considered "off the record."

2. Spoken words are considered "on the record."

3. Men are more likely than women to pay attention to "off the record" nonverbal behaviors.

Source: Copyright © 2012 by Audrey Nelson and Claire Damken Brown.

Debrief

The facilitator asks the group for their true or false responses to the three questions and asks follow-up questions to get the participants' reasons for their answers.

1. **True.** Many people think nonverbal behaviors are "off the record" and considered unimportant. They may not be tracked as easily as verbal messages during certain interactions such as depositions (considered "on the record"). "Because nonverbal cues are sent and received at a low level of awareness, we overlook and underestimate their power and importance" (Nelson, 2004, p. 3).

2. **True.** Spoken words or verbal statements are considered on the record. Words are easily recorded in e-mails, reports, statements, videotapes, and presentations. In general their interpretation remains fairly constant within a culture and by using that culture's or country's dictionary to find words' meanings.

3. **False.** We mentioned earlier in the chapter that women, not men, are more likely to pay attention to nonverbal behaviors and interpret them to add meaning to the broader messages. Women have a greater ability to self-monitor and read nonverbal messages. Women's socialization and status teaches them to nurture and care about others' feelings; therefore, women are more successful at attending to and interpreting facial expressions. Both women and men should pay attention to others' nonverbal behaviors as they add to the understanding of the whole message. More important, men and women should pay attention to their own nonverbal behaviors and strategically use these behaviors to complement their verbal messages.

Men and women: Be strategic and use nonverbal behaviors to complement verbal messages.

---

training tip

This chapter builds on past discussions that examined how boys and girls are socialized and learn "appropriate" male and female communication roles including nonverbal behaviors. This chapter may be combined with other chapters; use discussions from earlier in the book to look at how gender socialization affects adults' gender-appropriate nonverbal communication behaviors. Like the previous chapters, this chapter may also be used as a stand-alone program.

Exercise 4.4. Case Study: Something in the Way She Feels

Goal

Identify men's and women's responses to nonverbal behaviors.

Objectives

- Explore men's and women's ability to interpret nonverbal communication.

- Assign meaning and value to nonverbal communication.

Timing of Exercise

15 minutes total:

5 minutes to read the case and talk in small groups

10 minutes to hear the responses from each group or a sample of groups

Materials

Handout: Case Study: Something in the Way She Feels, chart paper and easel, markers

Optional: Create a slide to display the case study.

Setup

☐ Place participants in coed groups of five to eight.

☐ Ask each group to assign a scribe, who will take notes on the group's answers to the case study questions.

☐ The content for the handout includes the case study and questions. Distribute the handout and ask the participants to read it.

☐ Address each question with the entire class and ask for the individual group answers.

Case Study: Something in the Way She Feels

Maggie looked at Jon, then looked down and said, "I don't think the Software Extreme team is going to go for our proposal."

"Why would you say that? They didn't say anything bad. They said they'd think about it," replied Jon.

"It's not what they said. It was how they looked at each other when you were talking. There was something happening there. Did you see the team leader close his notebook and cross his arms when you started the slides?" Maggie said in a discouraged tone.

Jon countered emphatically, "You're way off on this one. I was there, too, you know. They asked some good questions. I didn't hear one negative thing from them."

Jon turned and started walking away.

"No," Maggie sighed. "We didn't get the job."

Source: Copyright © 2012 by Audrey Nelson and Claire Damken Brown.

Questions

1. What happened?

2. List Maggie's and Jon's behaviors and comments that helped and those that hurt the discussion.

3. Was gender a concern in this communication? How?

4. How would you have managed the discussion?

5. What could both parties do to improve the discussion?

Debrief

The facilitator requests feedback and discusses how the groups responded to the questions. Discuss the impact of nonverbal behaviors. The following are additional questions to ask the participants:

1. Was Maggie seeing more into the situation than warranted? Why or why not?

2. Why did Jon disagree with Maggie?

3. What role did nonverbal communication play in this situation?

Between words and behaviors, most people believe the behaviors. The nonverbal behaviors themselves are considered a truer reflection of our emotions than our words. "Nonverbal behavior is free of deception and distortion. It's hard to lie about our true intent because our nonverbals give us away" (Nelson, 2004, p. 3). And in U.S. culture we have sayings such as "walk the talk," "actions speak louder than words," and "seeing is believing." We have been taught to look at someone's actions and nonverbal messages to ensure that they reflect the person's words, that there is no mixed message.

Section 2: Gender Touch and Power at Work

Exercise 4.5. Learning Gender Touch: Touch the Girl and Not the Boy

Goal

Explore what men and women learn are appropriate touch behaviors.

Objectives

- Identify how boys and girls learn what is appropriate touching behavior.

- Understand how touch communicates various messages.

- Look at the rules of appropriate touch in the workplace.

Timing of Exercise

15 minutes

Materials

Handout: Appropriate or Inappropriate Touching, chart paper and easel, markers

Slide 4.5

Setup

☐ Conduct this exercise in dyads and then process it with the entire group, or ask the group as a whole the question and statement seen on the slide.

☐ Distribute the handout. The content for the handout is the same as the content on slide 4.5.

☐ Ask the group to respond to the question and statement.

☐ Ask the group for their responses and comments about the question and statement.

Slide 4.5

Appropriate or Inappropriate Touching

Is there such a thing as appropriate or inappropriate touching in the workplace? Provide three examples.

The three considerations of touch:

- How
- Where
- Why

Source: Copyright © 2012 by Audrey Nelson and Claire Damken Brown.

Debrief

Touch communicates many things, such as a congratulatory handshake, a consoling touch on the forearm, or a quick hug to say hello. At work, acceptable touching includes a handshake, which some consider the safest way to touch another at the office; a pat on the back is usually acceptable as long as it's a light touch on the back in the upper-shoulder area. A light touch on the forearm, a quick hug hello, or a quick kiss on the cheek as a greeting may be appropriate depending on your workplace and culture. In the United States and other countries that have various sexual harassment laws, employees do need to be aware of their company policies when touching other employees.

> Women learn that touch is a supportive
> and nurturing behavior.

Whether the person being touched is a man or a woman, employees need to consider how, where, and why they are touching another person at work. An individual should consider the reason for the touch. Does the touch show the dominance of the boss, the desired dominance of one colleague over another, sympathy at a friend's job loss, congratulations for the promotion, or a greeting? Where someone is touched includes where on that person's body (head, shoulder, butt, arm, or other area) and also where at work: in the boss's office, in the hallway in front of others, in the restroom, and so on. Even where your company is located, in terms of country and culture, will influence what is perceived as appropriate touch for men and women in the workplace. Each of these areas may communicate different messages. In U.S. culture when touch is reciprocal—that is, when it happens equally between two individuals—then it is usually viewed as touch happening between equals in the conversation. How one touches another should be considered in terms of the message imparted. What is communicated when a man uses a loose half-style handshake with another man? What is communicated when he uses a bone-breaking handshake with a woman?

To a great extent, touch reflects how men and women speak. We have mentioned that women tend to be relationship-oriented in their communication and men tend to be task- or goal-oriented. Young girls learn about cooperation and playing together. They learn to use touch to support and nurture, for instance, softly holding and caressing their baby doll, combing their doll's hair, holding hands, and walking arm-in-arm with other girls. Meanwhile young boys on the playground are learning about status and winning (meeting their goals). Their concept of touch is learned through behaviors such as pushing, shoving, hitting, wrestling, playing war, or roughhousing. They learn that being physical will help their status. To be seen as stronger than the others contributes to a boy's winning the task. Young girls learn to relate touch to connecting with others, while young boys don't receive that message (Payne, 2001, p. 136).

> Men learn that touch helps them achieve power and control.

Certainly there are little girls and boys who display the other gender's style of touch. When very young, this contradictory behavior may be ignored; but as a child gets older, there is a tendency for children and adults to ask the child to use behaviors that coincide with their biological sex. This is not right or wrong; it's a societal norm that we expect girls and women to act one way and boys and men to act another way. For example, some little girls may be viewed as "tomboys" when they use a rough-and-tumble playstyle. A little boy who wants to hold hands with other little boys may be viewed as a wimp. This expectation influences how we view gender-appropriate touch behaviors and carries over to the workplace.

Women and men also use the knowledge of someone's sex (male or female) to decide how and when to touch the other person. Payne (2001) mentions research that found that "parents tend to touch their sons less often and more roughly than their daughters. Daughters receive gentle, more protective touch from parents" (p. 136). Boys learn not to anticipate supportive nurturing touches; they learn touch means power and control (Wood, 2005, p. 137).

The concept of reciprocal touch indicates that two people who are touching each other in the same manner, such as a pat on the back or a touch on the forearm, shows that both parties support each other in an equal manner. Men do not touch each other as often as women touch other women. When women touch other women, it indicates friendship as part of their nurturing role (Gamble & Gamble, 2003, p. 99). Other research indicates that "women initiate hugs and touches expressing support, affection, and comfort; men use touch to direct others, assert power, and express sexual interest" (Payne, 2001, p. 136; Gamble & Gamble, 2003, p. 99).

Exercise 4.6. Touch, Power, and Perceived Power

Goal

Understand touch and power, in terms of nonverbal behaviors attributed to women and men.

Objectives

- Generate discussion from attendees about their experiences with touch and power-related nonverbal behaviors used by men and women.

- Create awareness of the impact of gender differences in terms of touch and power-related nonverbal behaviors.

Timing of Exercise

20 minutes total:

6 to 8 minutes to complete the true/false questions and discuss them with the group

12 to 14 minutes to get comments from individuals or from a sample of the groups

Materials

Handout: Touch, Power, and Perceived Power (Table 4.1), chart paper and easel, markers

Setup

☐ Complete this true/false exercise individually or in a group. Either have the participants complete the handout on their own and then form small coed groups of five to eight for discussion; or initially form groups of five to eight members in which members discuss and select their responses, and then process this with the entire group.

☐ As an alternative, start by forming groups and assign each group particular questions that they will decide are true or false and be responsible for discussing with the larger participant group.

☐ Ask the participants to indicate true or false for each item listed on the handout. If in small groups, ask the participants to discuss with the group members their reactions to the questions and their reasoning for selecting true or false.

☐ After six to eight minutes, get the group's attention and proceed with reviewing the true/false responses and the discussion.

☐ Distribute the handout.

Debrief

Below are facilitator questions for group processing and discussion points:

1. Which questions did the participants have trouble deciding whether they were true or false? Why?

2. How did they come to their decision (true or false)?

3. Would they share an example that relates to the question or statement?

Table 4.1. Touch, Power, and Perceived Power

True/False	Read each item and mark as T (True) or F (False):
	1. People with power tend to touch others of lesser power more often.
	2. People with power want to be physically touched by people they think have less power.
	3. Men: Generally touch women more often than women touch men.
	4. Men: Generally are viewed as having greater status and power than women.
	5. Women: Generally are more aware of touch, both being touched and touching others.
	6. The amount and type of touch changes as men and women get to know each other better and develop a friendship or collegial relationship.
	7. It is never appropriate for a male boss to touch a female subordinate.
	8. It is never appropriate for a female subordinate to touch a male boss.

Source: Copyright © 2012 by Audrey Nelson and Claire Damken Brown.

To reveal the correct true/false responses, the facilitator may choose to discuss the responses one by one, asking for comments or thoughts on each question. Or the facilitator may choose to reveal the correct true/false answers by displaying them on chart paper or on a slide and then ask for comments from the participants using the questions mentioned previously. For a large group of forty or more or an auditorium-sized group, the facilitator may ask the participants for a show of hands indicating whether a question is true or false. Then after the last question, open for discussion and ask the participants if they have any comments on a particular question.

1. **True.** People with greater power or status do tend to touch others with lesser power more often. The amount of touch is an indicator of dominance. In a work setting an individual who wants to show dominance will readily touch those she or he views as having less power or status. Some studies indicate that because men have

learned to associate touch with dominance and control, men touch others to demonstrate their power. People with higher status—whether age, experience, economic status, or race—touch others with lower status more frequently. Overall, people who touch others are viewed as having more power than those receiving the touch.

2. **False.** High-status people do not want to be touched by those whom they view as lower status than themselves. If a high-status person initiates touching someone of a lower status, the lower-status person generally does not reciprocate that touch (Payne, 2001, p. 136).

3. **True.** In terms of dominance, directing others, or sexual interest, men touch women and initiate touch more frequently than women (Gamble & Gamble, 2003, p. 99). Other research indicates that, in terms of nurturing behaviors, women initiate more hugs and embraces than men. When touching men, women also use touch to attempt control (p. 99).

4. **True.** In U.S. culture and many others, men are viewed as having more power and higher status than women. We see this in workplaces when female doctors are assumed to be nurses or male nurses are assumed to be doctors. It has happened frequently that the sole woman at a male-only executive meeting is assumed to be the secretary rather than the CEO. Interestingly, when it's a sole man at a staff meeting with all women, the man is still assumed to have higher status than the women present.

5. **True.** Women or any groups that are perceived as having lower status are more aware of being touched by others. Because they are more aware of being touched, they generally are more aware of how and when they touch others. Jones (1986) described "feminine-appropriate" touch and "masculine-inappropriate" touch. Since women are relationship-oriented, they have learned to view touch as nurturing and supportive, whether being touched or touching others: "touching is primarily a feminine-appropriate behavior" (p. 237). Jones thought that not only is women's touch more appropriate "but that

females touch more appropriately" than men (p. 239). If women's touch is considered appropriate and nurturing behavior, then men may see their touch as inappropriate and tend to use touch less often (p. 239). This is contrary to other findings and discussion that indicated men touch women more often than women touch men.

6. **True.** At the beginning of a collegial relationship men tend to touch more, and as the friendship develops, women begin to touch others more. Regarding work relations, this is seen as the team members get to know each other better. Women become more at ease with initiating touch toward men and reciprocating men's touch (Gamble & Gamble, 2003, p. 100).

7. **False.** Certainly there are appropriate times for touching at work: handshakes, a pat on the back, a brief touch on the forearm, and so on. When touch is knowingly used to dominate the other person, whether male or female, then that behavior's correctness is questioned. If the male boss is using that touch as a sexual overture, that touch needs to be questioned in terms of the manager's responsibility, company policy such as dating a subordinate and supervisor liability, and keeping the environment free of any potential sexual harassment.

8. **False.** As previously mentioned, there are appropriate times for touching at work: handshakes, a pat on the back, a brief touch on the forearm, and so on. If the female subordinate intends the touch to be a sexual overture to her male boss, then she needs to be aware of any company policy regarding workplace dating, especially dating one's boss.

What happens when a woman touches a male colleague of equal or lesser status than she? Gamble and Gamble (2003) noted that in the workplace men and women are often competitors and that "men tend to respond negatively to being touched by women considered to be of equal status; men do not respond negatively, however, if they perceive the women to be of higher status" (p. 100). So we see that touch weaves an interesting workplace web between power, women, and men.

Exercise 4.7. Her and His First Impressions

Goal

Explore the nonverbal aspects of first impressions.

Objectives

- Learn three key nonverbal behaviors that affect women's and men's first impressions.

- Understand how to improve first impressions through nonverbal behaviors.

Timing of Exercise

15 minutes

Materials

Chart paper and easel, markers

Slide 4.6

Setup

☐ Conduct this exercise in dyads and then process it with the entire group or ask the group as a whole the question and statement seen on the slide.

☐ Ask the groups to identify three critical connections affecting a first impression as requested on the slide.

☐ After four to five minutes, discuss the groups' responses and comments.

Slide 4.6

Her and His First Impressions

People form a first impression through three critical connections:

1.

2.

3.

Source: Copyright © 2012 by Audrey Nelson and Claire Damken Brown.

Debrief

First impressions are formed quickly and tend to remain unchanged. Quick decisions are made based on your nonverbal messages from frown to smile, clothing, haircut, briefcase, or visible piercings, tattoos, and other body modifications. Research has shown that decisions about trustworthiness, aggressiveness, likeability, attractiveness, and competence have been made in as little as one hundred milliseconds—that's a tenth of a second (Willis & Todorov, 2006, p. 592). In a series of experiments examining facial appearance and first impressions, participants viewed unfamiliar faces for either a tenth of a second, half a second, or one second and rated them in terms of particular traits. With a longer time of one second, trait judgments generally stayed the same. Regarding this study with student researcher Janine Willis, Princeton University professor Alexander Todorov commented, "What we found was that, if given more time, people's fundamental judgment about faces did not change. Observers simply became more confident in their judgments as the duration lengthened" (Boutin, 2006).

First impressions are formed quickly and
tend to remain unchanged.

When first meeting someone, men and women make three critical connections that influence their first impression of an individual: eye contact, smile, and handshake ("Making a great first impression," n.d.; Nelson, 2004, p. 100; and C. Brown & Nelson, 2009, p. 98). Ask the participants if they agree or disagree that these three items are critical for forming first impressions and why.

In a business setting, meeting someone for the first time calls for direct eye contact in U.S. culture. In this situation, eye contact signifies honesty, trustworthiness, and competence for both men and women. However, if a person looks away, such as a darting glance to the side, the person may be viewed as being less trustworthy and somewhat deceptive. If two people initially have eye contact while shaking hands and then one party lowers her or his eyes, this is interpreted as submissive behavior. Lowering one's eyes is considered a lower status and "less than" behavior. Women tend to use the lowering of eyes as a submissive move or display of acquiescence. When meeting or shaking hands with a man, if a woman lowers her eyes she will be confirmed as the lower-status person or person with less authority. In business settings, especially those that are male-dominated, women tend to already be viewed as lower status when compared to men. It's recommended that women be aware of their eye contact and the level of authority they want to portray when meeting others.

Men's eye contact is key during a handshake, whether shaking hands with women or men. During a handshake, men usually have direct eye contact. They tend to use their eye contact as an indicator of superiority or higher status. As the two men look into each other's eyes, the man who breaks eye contact first may be considered as being submissive or having less authority. The man or woman who fails this stare down is thought to be in a one-down position. In addition to the handshake ritual, this type of eye contact can also be seen at business meetings, performance discussions, or even walking down the hallway. When a woman and a man are walking toward each other in the hallway, what happens? If they look at each other for an equal amount of time, then it may be perceived that they are equals. If one looks down or physically gets out of the way of the other, the one who got out of the way is viewed as the lower-status person (usually the woman).

Smiling is a universal indication of friendliness and welcoming another in a greeting. A smile is important in that initial meeting to indicate openness when greeting the other person. This is true for both women and men. When meeting someone for the first time, a smile is needed to create a good first impression; it adds to the perception of trustworthiness. Sometimes women may smile too often or incongruently; sometimes men may not smile at all. However, during that first meeting and handshake, it is appropriate for men and women to smile to create a welcoming, friendly atmosphere and a positive first impression.

> Women tend to use the lowering of eyes as a submissive move or display of acquiescence.

Shaking hands with a colleague is one of the few legitimate forms of touch in the workplace. It may be the "only sanctioned" touch behavior in the office (C. Brown & Nelson, 2009, p. 99). Even a pat on the back may be questioned if that pat borders on a rub. The handshake is a custom in which both men and women should participate. The handshake serves as a tool that begins to build the relationship between two individuals. The touch of the handshake contributes to relationship building in the same manner as a welcoming hug. However, in many workplaces hugs are off limits. Men may very well have the advantage in the workplace when it comes to the handshake. Since they were little boys, they have been trained to extend their arm and grasp the other's hand for a firm full-palm handshake. The handshake is a business custom that some may say is outdated, but that touching formality still is a valuable bonding opportunity to build camaraderie. It's considered a business touch and not an intimacy touch.

The handshake can take different forms such as weak, "the crusher," sweaty palms, and "dead fish." The custom of the handshake stems from the male business world (Nelson, 2004, pp. 138–139). A masculine handshake may be used at times for power and dominance. A "Professional Sales Tips" online site gives a prescription for a power handshake for men. It provides instructions on how to deliver an intimidating "power handshake" to show "that you are confident, in control, and not afraid to use it" (S. Brown, 1999). Women would not design a "how-to" on power handshakes. The website suggests extending the right hand slightly tilted to the right, grasp their hand, have your palm and webbing by the thumb touching the other's webbing. Then turn your hand to the left so your hand is now horizontal on top, and squeeze firmly. It states to squeeze "really hard if you are greeting a competitor"; this type of handshake shows dominance. Others suggest that extending your hand open with palm face up is an indication that you are open and not threatened by the other person.

Some women may have learned that they do not have to shake hands at all, while some men may have learned that they do not have to shake hands with a woman, unless she extends her hand first. The nonverbal message of the handshake is that of a business-level equalizer. It brings women and men together in an approved workplace touch ritual that starts building that bonding relationship that women seek. Women need to shake hands on a regular basis with both men and women. Likewise, men need to extend their hand to greet women, in addition to men. To shake hands, look at the other person, extend your arm, keep your hand vertical, and use the full palm for a firm grasp (C. Brown & Nelson, 2009, p. 99).

Women and men: Shake hands. Use a
firm full-palm handshake.

Can that first impression be changed? "'As time passes and you get to
know people, you, of course, develop a more rounded conception of
them,' Todorov said. 'But because we make these judgments without
conscious thought, we should be aware of what is happening when we
look at a person's face'" (Boutin, 2006). If the first impression stems
from a job interview and the person does not get the job, then
Todorov's suggestion to get to know the person better to change that
first impression won't happen. To get that job it's imperative for men
and women to create a positive impression the first time around.

Section 3: Space: The Final Gender Frontier

Exercise 4.8. Space Rules, Power, and Status

Goal

Discover how women and men use space to influence power and status.

Objectives

- Understand men's and women's use of space and its impact on the
  workplace.

- Identify gender differences in how women and men use space.

Timing of Exercise

15 minutes

Materials

Handout: Space Rules, Power, and Status, chart paper and easel, markers
Slide 4.7

Setup

☐ Either conduct this exercise in dyads and then process it with the entire group, or conduct it in groups of five to eight members, in which each member shares his or her response, and then process it with the entire group.

☐ Ask the participants to take a few minutes to read the statements, fill in the blanks, and compare their responses within the group.

☐ After about seven to eight minutes, reconvene as a larger group and ask the participants how they completed each statement. Ask the groups to share any comments or discussion points raised in their small-group discussions.

☐ Distribute the handout.

Slide 4.7

Space Rules, Power, and Status

When sitting in a room, think of space as power: the more space you demand, the more powerful you may be perceived.

Source: Copyright © 2012 by Audrey Nelson and Claire Damken Brown.

Sample Handout Text: Space Rules, Power, and Status

Complete these sentences using *women* or *men*. Each word may be used more than once.

1. Studies have shown that _____ invade _____'s space more than _____ invade _____'s space.

2. When challenged for that space by men or women, _____ generally give up the space or just leave instead of defending the area; _____ tend to defend their space.

3. When walking down the hallway, _____ are more likely to move out of the way of someone; while _____ are less likely to move out of the way of someone.

4. _____ have a smaller personal space than _____.

5. _____ expand their space by pushing out their chests and sitting with their legs spread wide open.

(*Source:* C. Brown & Nelson, 2009; Gamble & Gamble, 2003; Wood, 2005.)

Debrief

Share the following correct answers with the participants. Discuss any participants' comments and questions. Ask the participants if they have any examples they'd like to share related to these statements.

1. Studies have shown that <u>men</u> invade <u>women's</u> space more than <u>women</u> invade <u>men</u>'s space.

2. When challenged for that space by men or women, <u>women</u> generally give up the space or just leave instead of defending the area; <u>men</u> tend to defend their space.

3. When walking down the hallway, <u>women</u> are more likely to move out of the way of someone; while <u>men</u> are less likely to move out of the way of someone.

4. <u>Women</u> have a smaller personal space than <u>men</u>.

5. <u>Men</u> expand their space by pushing out their chests and sitting with their legs spread wide open.

The study of the meaning of space and distance is referred to as *proxemics*. Edward Hall, an anthropologist, coined the term *proxemics* in the 1960s and is considered the father of the field. Hall's intercultural interactions led him "to believe that basic differences in the way that members of different cultures perceived reality were responsible for miscommunications of the most fundamental kind" (N. Brown,

2001). Part of that reality focused on the use of space and distance that formed cultural patterns indicating how close people got when interacting. The more familiar a person was with the culture's use of space and distance, then the better able that person would be to communicate and maneuver within that culture. Through the use of space and distance, power and status are revealed. In U.S. culture, the more space a person has (think of that limousine or Hummer), then the more power or status that person is perceived to have. The boss may have the corner office, but the CEO has the top floor penthouse: more square footage equals more power and higher status. Proxemics studies by Spain and Weissman (as cited in Wood, 2005, p. 135) indicate a "lesser status for women and minorities" in the United States.

> When sitting in a room, think of space as power:
> The more space you command, the more powerful
> you may be perceived as being.

Space and distance are indicators of men's and women's power and status in U.S. culture. Space and distance patterns reflect women's and men's power and status. The higher-status person tends to be the man; therefore, the man is granted or is entitled to more space and distance when interacting with the perceived lower-status women. Someone having higher status and power is permitted to infringe on the space of someone of lesser status and power (for example, the male boss can invade his female subordinate's space). The reverse is viewed as inappropriate and as an invasion of the high-status person's space (for example, it tends not to be acceptable for a female subordinate to invade her male boss's space). Because being male carries with it a perception of higher status, a male subordinate may be able to invade the space of his female boss; however, this is not advisable because the boss is still the boss and may expect the same courtesies and respect that would be extended to anyone of high status.

Women tend to give up their space more willingly than men. Again if we look at status levels, people at a lower status tend to yield their space to the person with higher status. When the boss enters the conference room and needs a chair, the tendency is for someone of a lower-level job, such as a secretary or clerk, to stand and present his or her chair to the boss. Likewise, when walking down the corridor, the woman will stand to the side or get out of the way of the man coming toward her usually before the man motions that he will move out of her way.

> Women tend to give up their space more
> willingly than men.

The lower-status person, the woman, generally takes up less space while the higher-status person, the man, takes up more space. Women have been socialized to be relationship oriented. A woman will give up her space or move aside in an effort to maintain the relationship with the other person. Men have learned gestures and body movements that take up space as examples of dominance, competitiveness, power, and winning. Taking up space nonverbally communicates that he is the winner ("I got the corner office"; "I have my own parking space"). Women tend to make themselves smaller (sit with arms crossed, legs crossed, or move out of the way), partly as a function of taking up less space as a lower-status person and having a smaller personal space than men (Wood, 2005, pp. 135–136; C. Brown & Nelson, 2009, p. 102). In general, women or others who want to show their power could adopt some of the dominance behaviors, such as using more space at the conference table and sitting with arms uncrossed and legs uncrossed.

Exercise 4.9. Who Are the Space Invaders: Women or Men?

Goal

Examine women's and men's comfort levels with personal space.

Objectives

- Discuss the relationship between personal space, gender, and status.

- Encourage individuals to experiment with their comfort level for personal space.

Timing of Exercise

15 minutes

Materials

Chart paper and easel, markers

Slide 4.8

Setup

☐ Conduct this exercise in dyads and then process it with the entire group. The exercise works best when participants number twenty or more and there is enough space to move around in the room.

☐ Ask individuals to find partners for this exercise. If there are an uneven number of participants, have the extra individual act as an observer of a particular dyad.

☐ Once participants have selected their partners, ask them to stand facing each other, approximately ten feet apart, and with no barriers between them. If an individual is unable to stand, ask them to sit comfortably ten feet away and face their selected partner.

☐ Tell the pairs to pick one person who will stand still and one who will move.

☐ Tell them at the word *go,* one person will start moving toward the other until the other person says *stop.* Tell them to freeze where they are.

☐ *Note:* Some dyads will be two men, two women, or a woman and a man.

Slide 4.8

WHO ARE THE SPACE INVADERS:
Women or Men?

Find a partner. Listen for further instructions.

What's a comfortable distance?

What's an uncomfortable distance?

Source: Copyright © 2012 by Audrey Nelson and Claire Damken Brown.

---

training tip

If there is an uneven number of participants when an exercise calls for dyads, have the extra individual act as an observer of a particular group. The observer may simply observe the interaction and provide comments and feedback to the dyad members.

Debrief

With the participants in their frozen positions, ask them to look around the room. There will be same-sex and mixed-sex dyads. Note that the women dyads are usually standing the closest. Then the mixed-sex dyads are next in terms of standing close. The farthest apart are usually the men dyads.

Ask the participants for their comfortable conversation distance; chart these responses. Ask the participants for the "too close for comfort" stopping point; chart these responses. Discuss with the participants how they felt for each stopping point. Time permitting, the facilitator may get responses from both parties in the dyad. The facilitator may follow up by asking:

1. How did you feel at the stopping point?

2. What made you think that the stopping point was a good distance or was getting too close?

3. Did you ever feel that your space was being invaded? When? Why?

4. In terms of distance, would it make any difference to you if your partner were of the same sex or the opposite sex?

Gamble and Gamble (2003, p. 101) comment that women's personal space tends to be "smaller than the personal bubble that surrounds a man. Because the stereotype is that women are more social, more affiliative, and of lower status than men, the space surrounding women is perceived to be more public and therefore viewed as more accessible than the space surrounding men." Men tend to be more sensitive and disapproving when the space invasion comes from the front; women tend to be more sensitive and disapproving when it comes from the side (Fisher & Byrne as cited in Gamble & Gamble, 2003, p. 101). In addition to status differences influencing distance, homophobia may affect men's comfort level, with them preferring a larger same-sex personal space than women. U.S. culture generally has no taboos questioning women's sexual orientation when two women are standing close to each other in social settings. With an assumption that heterosexuality is "the norm," two men who are strangers to each other may keep their distance and stand farther apart, fearing that their sexual orientation may be questioned if they are standing too close (or as close as two women would stand).

Women's personal space is smaller than
men's personal space.

The generally accepted social distance for conversation in the United States is four to seven feet. Hall suggested that eighteen inches was usually an appropriate personal space in the United States (N. Brown, 2001). In other countries conversational distance is much less. For example, in some Middle Eastern countries, when speaking with a colleague, one is expected to feel the other person's breath on one's face. The sense of maintaining personal space varies by culture and status level. As people in the United States stand closer to each other, if they are strangers they will want to maintain their personal distance or space, also referred to as their personal bubble. To keep that bubble around them, they may start moving away or backward from the person they think is infringing on their space. As a friendship with a colleague develops, the size of the personal space is reduced, as the individual grants approval for that space invasion.

Section 4: Something in the Way She and He Move: Women's and Men's Gestures and Movements

Gestures and body movements, also called *kinesics,* are affected by power and status. Similar to personal space, men and women need to be cognizant of how and when they use certain gestures and how they may affect others' perceptions of their power and status. See Table 4.2 for general differences between men's and women's gestures that tend to be perceived as dominance or submissiveness when communicating with the opposite sex.

Table 4.2. Women's and Men's Movements

Women's Movements: Submissiveness	Men's Movements: Dominance
Use less body space and condense themselves	Use large sweeping gestures and expand
Pull in their bodies, stand with legs close together	Sit in outstretched positions, stand with legs apart in a wide stance
Tilt head	Keep head straight
Keep their arms close to their bodies, cross arms in front	Hold their arms away from their bodies
Hold their hands in their own laps	Stretch their hands out
Cross their legs at the knees, often twisting their ankles too (a double wrap)	Sit with their legs open
Sit on the edge of the chair	Lean back in the chair
Give up space	Take more space, spread out
May have more eye contact when listening	May stare more, may look and glance away
May lower eyes	Point more, stroke chin more

Source: Adapted from Payne, 2001, pp. 134–135.

When men and women are communicating with each other, it is important to be aware of these nonverbal behaviors and their impact on the messages you send. A woman's behavior of tilting her head may seem subtle; nonetheless, it can undermine perceptions of her authority. A man who lowers his eyes and doesn't participate in the stare down may be perceived as not a leader. Women and men are advised to be aware of their messages and use nonverbal messages congruent with their verbal messages.

Exercise 4.10. Her and His Facial Expressions

Goal

Learn about messages from men's and women's facial expressions.

Objectives

- Develop an awareness of the face's nonverbal messages.

- Identify gender differences and similarities in the use of facial expressions.

Timing of Exercise

15 minutes

Materials

Handout: Her and His Facial Expressions, chart paper and easel, markers

Slide 4.9

Setup

☐ Use this exercise as a way to get the participants thinking about how men and women use their faces to express themselves.

☐ Conduct the exercise in dyads and process it with the entire group, or conduct it in groups of five to eight members, in which each member shares his or her response, and then process it with the entire group.

☐ Distribute the handout.

Slide 4.9

FACIAL EXPRESSIONS: Something to Consider

"Faces are our best window into other people's hearts."

Source: Conniff, 2004, p. 50.

Sample Handout Text: Her and His Facial Expressions

The face is a plentiful source of information.

Complete these sentences using *women* or *men*. Each word may be used more than once.

1. _____ tend to display more facial expressions than _____.

2. _____ tend to interpret facial expressions more accurately than _____.

3. _____ tend to smile more often than _____.

4. _____ seem to smile more often whether they are happy or sad, confident or afraid.

5. If _____ smile too much, it begins to affect their credibility.

6. _____ tend to mask or hide their emotions.

7. Those who have power and status, usually _____ in most workplaces, don't need to smile.

8. When _____ and _____ smile, it tends to make others smile, too.

Answer Key

1. <u>Women</u> tend to display more facial expressions than <u>men</u>.

2. <u>Women</u> tend to interpret facial expressions more accurately than <u>men</u>.

3. <u>Women</u> tend to smile more often than <u>men</u>.

4. <u>Women</u> seem to smile more often whether they are happy or sad, confident or afraid.

5. If <u>women</u> smile too much, it begins to affect their credibility.

6. <u>Men</u> tend to mask or hide their emotions.

7. Those who have power and status, usually <u>men</u> in most workplaces, don't need to smile.

8. When <u>men</u> and <u>women</u> smile, it tends to encourage others around them to smile, too.

Source: Adapted from C. Brown & Nelson, 2009, p. 105.

Debrief

Here is something to consider: "Faces are our best window into other people's hearts" (Conniff, 2004, p. 50). Earlier in this chapter, smiling was discussed as a positive connection when making a first impression. A smile can show acknowledgment or agreement. Since women are the relationship builders, they learn to use their facial expressions to show support and share their emotions with others. Because women tend to use a lot of facial expressions, in the workplace they are sometimes labeled as overanimated: "Why does Allison get so excited about everything? She needs to calm down." Men have learned to hide their emotions and facial expressions, perhaps in an attempt to keep the upper hand by not letting their guard down. Men's controlled approach to their emotions leads others to think that they are levelheaded: "Bill is unflappable. He's got his act together. He plays it cool." When in the side-by-side stance men tend to use when talking with each other, they may make less effort to use facial expressions since those expressions are not readily seen when the men are not directly facing each other.

Men: Masking or hiding your emotions when talking with women may contribute to women viewing you as unresponsive, uncaring, and not listening.

Exercise 4.11. The Strong Silent Type

Goal

Explore silence as a nonverbal tool.

Objectives

- Get the groups talking about men's and women's silent behaviors in the workplace.

- Identify the meaning of women's and men's different types of silent behaviors.

Timing of Exercise

15 minutes

Materials

Handout: The Silent Behaviors of Men and Women, chart paper and easel, markers

Setup

☐ Conduct this exercise in dyads and process it with the entire group, or conduct it in groups of five to eight members, where each member shares his or her response, and then process it with all the participants.

☐ Distribute the handout.

Sample Handout Text: The Silent Behaviors of Men and Women

1. Is silence "golden"?

2. How is silence a conversation tool?

3. Do the words *strong silent type* refer to a man or a woman? Why?

4. What does silence say about a man?

5. What does silence say about a woman?

6. How do these perceptions affect men and women at work?

Source: Copyright © 2012 by Audrey Nelson and Claire Damken Brown.

Debrief

With no words a message may be expressed through silence. When silent, men are generally perceived as intelligent, thoughtful, and strong—as in the "strong silent type." Keeping one's mouth shut and not immediately blurting out words in response to a question often gives the impression that the person is taking time to consider the appropriate response before speaking. This can be a positive behavior for men and women.

When asking a question, silence can be used as a positive conversational tool. If a person asks a question and chooses to wait in silence for a response, that silence often makes the responder feel as if he or she needs to talk to fill in that seemingly awkward silent gap. This is a technique interrogators use and is often seen on television detective programs. The interrogator asks the suspect a question and then waits in silence until the suspect gets uncomfortable and starts sharing more information than he or she probably intended to fill in that silent gap.

When a woman is silent in meetings, the perception may be that she is not intelligent, not interested, in over her head, "unable to do the work," or not serious about her career. The issues for many women are the messages they heard when growing up, such as "it's better to be seen than heard, to speak only when spoken to," and being loud is not ladylike (C. Brown & Nelson, 2009, p. 110). Because of this socialization, women's silence in the U.S. workplace tends not to be considered a positive trait. In other countries, such as Japan, there is a greater acceptance of silence between two people talking; there is no rush to talk to fill in the silent gap.

The Voice's Message

Loud, soft, high pitch, low pitch, breathiness, inflection, rate of speech, and enunciation are examples of paralinguistic behavior or paralanguage that influences perceptions of spoken messages. Physical differences create the woman's high pitch, such as smaller, thinner vocal folds of the larynx when compared with a man's larger, thicker folds, and his larger pharynx, giving him lower tones (Wood, 2005, p. 139; Payne, 2001, p. 137).

> Women: Raising your pitch at the end of a sentence may lower your credibility in the workplace. Monitor your phrasing and lower your pitch at the statement's end.

Women's and men's vocal cues reflect their socialization. Women's voices are often softer, sounding more submissive or deferential when conversing with men; men's voices are often directive, louder, and authoritative, sounding strong, confident, and forceful. Women use more inflections to the point of making statements sound like questions, raising their pitch at the sentence's end: "The report will be done Friday?" or "The numbers you gave me were final?" This raised pitch at the end of the sentence may be interpreted by a male colleague as the woman being unsure of herself, thus lowering her credibility.

The man with the lower-pitched voice tends to be viewed as intelligent, mature, and manly. A female with a high-pitched voice tends to be seen as less intelligent, good looking, feminine, and immature (Wood, 2005, p. 140). Other research demonstrated that "women with breathy, small, tense voices are judged as pretty, feminine, petite, shallow, immature, and unintelligent. Men with throaty tense voices . . . are judged as mature, masculine, intelligent, and sophisticated" (Addington as cited in Payne, 2001, p. 139). A somewhat extreme example of how vocal pitch and tone influence messages and perceptions is acting icon Marilyn Monroe. Her whispery, singsong voice contributed to her movie image as being sexy or even overly sexual, unintelligent, and in need of a man's care; this image carried over to her personal life, too. The message for both men and women is to be aware of their voices and how they use them to create credible office images. The voice is one characteristic that can be changed with training to project the desired image.

Use the Action Steps slides (on pages 132 and 133) for men and women as part of your summary for the material you presented from this chapter.

Slide 4.10

Action Steps for Men

When talking with women . . .

- Be aware that masking facial expressions may make women feel that you are not accessible or responsive to their communications.

- Incorporate more nonverbal behaviors that facilitate interpersonal communication and interest:

  o Head nods

  o Nonfluencies (um, uh-huh, yeah)

  o Leaning forward

  o Facial animation

  o Eye contact

- Monitor nonverbal behaviors that may be overpowering.

- Be aware of how and when you challenge others, especially women, with a stare.

- Shake hands with your men and women business colleagues. Do not shake hands with only the men; offer your hand to women.

- Use a firm handshake and not the "bone crusher."

Source: Copyright © 2012 by Audrey Nelson and Claire Damken Brown.

Slide 4.11

Action Steps for Women

When talking with men . . .

- Monitor the potentially less-credible nonverbal behaviors you send:

  o Excessive smiling

  o Rising vocal pitch at the ends of sentences

  o Too high a pitch when speaking in general

  o Tilt of the head

- Be aware of "double messages" that are contradictions between the verbal and nonverbal messages (saying one thing and acting out a different message nonverbally).

- Assume more powerful nonverbal behaviors:

  o Using convincing tones

  o Incorporating gestures

  o Taking up space (don't shrink)

  o Using volume

- Shake hands with your men and women business colleagues. Offer your hand to women and men.

- Use a firm handshake and not the "limp fish."

Source: Copyright © 2012 by Audrey Nelson and Claire Damken Brown.

CHAPTER 5

How She and He Listen

Though neither sex may listen "better," it appears that women and men listen differently.

—Judy Pearson (1985, p. 162)

Learning Objectives

- Understand the differences in how women and men listen.

- Explore how the differences in men's and women's listening behaviors affect conversations and credibility.

- Suggest action steps for men and women to improve their skills when listening to each other.

Introduction

Listening often takes the back seat when it comes to talking about communicating successfully. As Claire mentions to her students, we need to listen louder than we speak to keep the peace. That includes listening to keep the peace between men and women in the workplace. While employees may spend hours learning how to give a presentation, how to get a message across, or what words to use to captivate the audience, they seldom address each person's responsibility to listen and hear—yes, actually hear—what the speaker is saying.

Many a woman has fallen victim to the get-him-to-listen syndrome. She thinks, "What do I have to do to get heard at this staff meeting? Stand on my head? Bring coffee and doughnuts?" (We advise not bringing the coffee and doughnuts to the meeting unless there's an agreement that team members—men and women—alternate bringing the snacks.) Learning a few things about the communication dynamics between men and women will help both groups start to listen and hear each other's messages. Men lament that when asking a woman a "simple" yes-or-no question, she will talk for hours about seemingly useless information and never get to the yes-or-no response for which the man desperately was hoping. He turns off his listening mode, completely satisfied that she's mumbling about totally irrelevant information. She may be no better as she listens intently to his every syllable, looking for each possible feeling that he may display. Then she may wonder sometimes for hours what he really meant and whether he was telling her everything, replaying the conversation in her head over and over again, determining the impact of his words on her relationship with him. By learning to listen to each other, women and men can make definite improvements in their communication.

Timing for Unit

1 hour and 15 minutes to 1 hour and 30 minutes

Materials for Unit

Handouts, chart paper and easel, markers

Slides 5.1 through 5.10

Section 1: Listening Between Him and Her

training tip

This chapter on listening builds on past discussions that examined how boys and girls are socialized and learn "appropriate" male and female communication roles. This chapter may be combined with other chapters; use the previous discussions to look at how gender socialization affects adults' interaction styles while discussing the impact of gender communication on how we listen. Like the previous chapters, this chapter may also be used as a stand-alone program.

Exercise 5.1. Start the Conversation: How She and He Listen

Goal

Begin a conversation about how women and men listen.

Objectives

- Get the groups talking about men's and women's listening behaviors in the workplace.

- Begin to identify gender differences in listening styles.

Timing of Exercise

10–15 minutes

Materials

Chart paper and easel, markers

Slide 5.1

Setup

☐ Use this exercise as a warm-up to get the audience thinking about their perceptions of how men and women listen to each other.

☐ Either conduct this exercise in dyads and process it with the entire group, or organize it in groups of five to eight members, in which each member shares his or her response, and then process it with the entire group.

☐ Ask the participants to read the statement on the slide and then talk with their group to respond to the two questions listed.

☐ Tell the participants they will have five minutes for discussion within their groups. Then selected groups will share their key points with the larger audience. Note that if it's a small group of twelve to eighteen people, you may have time to hear from each small group. If it's a larger group of twenty-five or more or an auditorium setting, the facilitator may have time to hear from only a few groups.

☐ After five minutes, get the group's attention and ask for a summary from each group (or from a few sample groups depending on the audience size).

Slide 5.1

START THE CONVERSATION:
How She and He Listen

Men hear with their ears. Women hear with their ears and eyes.

Source: C. Brown & Nelson, p. 58.

What does this statement mean to you?

How might it affect your behavior at work? Provide examples.

Debrief

This discussion serves as a brief introduction to examining listening behaviors. While listening to the groups reporting on their conversations, keep track of comments that relate to the upcoming discussions about differences in how men and women listen. If it is helpful, write significant comments on the chart and easel for future reference. When responding to the first question, participants will be describing what the statements mean to them, in terms of how men hear words or content and women hear the words and feelings behind the words. With the second question, attendees begin to think about their own listening styles and how these gender differences may have affected them in the workplace.

Exercise 5.2. His and Her Listening Behaviors

Goal

Explore the different listening behaviors of women and men.

Objectives

- Discuss the differences in men's and women's listening behaviors.

- Discover what participants think they know about how men and women listen.

- Generate awareness of gender differences in listening as it relates to self-disclosure.

Timing of Exercise

20–30 minutes

Materials

Chart paper and easel, markers

Slide 5.2

Setup

☐ Conduct this exercise in dyads and process it with the entire group, or organize it in groups of five to eight members, in which each member shares his or her response, and then process it with the entire group.

☐ Ask the participants to read the statement on the slide and then talk with their group to respond to the two questions listed.

☐ Tell the participants that they will have five minutes to discuss the statement within their groups, and then selected groups will share their key points with the larger audience. Note that if the total group size is twelve to eighteen people, you may have time to hear from each small group. If it's a larger group of twenty-five or more or an auditorium setting, you may only have time to hear from a few groups.

☐ After five minutes, get the entire group's attention and ask for a summary from each small group (or from a few sample groups depending on the audience size).

☐ It may be helpful to chart the participants' responses to the questions and compare them to the discussions later in the chapter.

Slide 5.2

His and Her Listening Behaviors

1. How are the behaviors different if it's a man listening versus a woman listening?

2. Who are better listeners: women or men? Why?

3. Do people most often choose to self-disclose to men or women? Why?

Source: Copyright © 2012 by Audrey Nelson and Claire Damken Brown.

Debrief

The participants explore listening skills and discuss observations of what they've experienced in how men and women listen. Discussion questions are used for their own self-reflection on their behaviors and perceptions. The questions have specific answers that are revealed throughout this chapter. The facilitator may comment on these questions in terms of what the research has shown; then indicate that the questions on the slide will be addressed further as the chapter continues.

1. When discussing the responses to the first question on the slide, see Table 5.1 for the general differences between men's and women's listening behaviors.

2. Referring to the second question on the slide, women tend to be perceived as better and more attentive listeners than men. See the explanations to true/false questions 6 and 10 in Exercise 5.5, How Women and Men Listen, that follows.

3. Referring to the third question on the slide, men and women prefer disclosing personal information to women rather than

Table 5.1. Men's and Women's Listening Behaviors

Men's Listening Behaviors	Women's Listening Behaviors
Hear the words and the content.	Hear the words and the emotions or feelings behind the words.
Goal-oriented, aim to solve the problem, prefer that the speaker get to the point.	Process-oriented, aim to gather information from all of the speaker's channels and review (generally more than once) before making a decision.
Decide quickly based on the content they hear.	Take longer to decide since they may want to gather more information and discuss it more than once to reach a decision.
Stand indirectly, side by side.	Stand face-to-face, looking at the person's face.
Take in the speaker's words to determine the message's meaning.	Take in all the speaker's behaviors (facial expression, tone of voice, and so on) connected to the message to determine the meaning.
Sometimes perceived as not listening due to side-by-side stance or not looking at the speaker.	Acknowledges the speaker by head nodding, looking at the speaker, saying "uh-huh" or making short comments such as "I agree" or "That makes sense."
Interrupts more often, which contributes to being perceived as not being a good listener.	Interrupts less often, which contributes to being perceived as being a better listener.

Source: Copyright © 2012 by Audrey Nelson and Claire Damken Brown.

men. See the explanation to true/false question 2 in Exercise 5.5, How Women and Men Listen, that follows.

Attendees may find themselves confronting their own stereotypes and expectations for how men and women should listen and talk with each other. As the facilitator, be aware that some audience members may disagree with you on generalizations about how men and women show they are listening to each other. After this exercise the audience will be ready to learn more about men's and women's listening styles and what men and women each can do to improve the quality of their listening.

If the training is taking place in front of a large group in an auditorium setting or in a setting where it may be hard for people to move their chairs closer to talk within a small group, the facilitator may choose to use dyads and instruct the attendees to turn and talk with their neighbor.

Exercise 5.3. Listening: Women Versus Men

Goal

Explore perceptions: Is one listening style better than another?

Objectives

- Discover what participants think about the benefits of women's and men's listening styles.

- Discuss the differences in how men and women may respond when listening to each other.

Timing of Exercise

8 minutes

Materials

Chart paper and easel, markers

Slide 5.3

Setup

☐ Either conduct this exercise in dyads and then process it with the entire group, or conduct it in groups of five to eight members, in which each member shares his or her response, and then process it with the entire group.

☐ Ask the participants to read the statements on the slide and then talk with their group to respond to the question listed.

☐ At four minutes, get the group's attention and proceed with asking for a summary from each group (or from a few sample groups depending on the audience size).

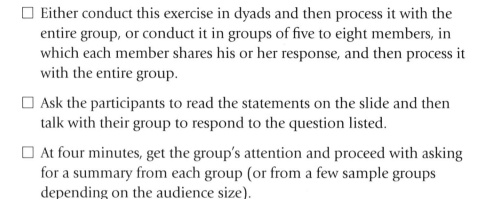

Slide 5.3

LISTENING: Women Versus Men

Who is right and who is wrong?

• Women hear feelings.

• Men hear facts.

• Mr. Fix-It or Ms. Empathetic?

Source: Copyright © 2012 by Audrey Nelson and Claire Damken Brown.

Debrief

In an earlier chapter we mentioned that men tend to be task- or goal-oriented in their approach to communication. Women tend to be process-oriented. How does this play out in terms of their listening? Men are listening for the content or words so that they can take action, make a quick decision, fix the situation (like Mr. Fix-It), close the topic, and move on to the next issue. They want to complete the task, solve the problem, and check it off the list. Done; move on (C. Brown & Nelson, 2009, pp. 55–56).

Women want to share their story with all its details so that the listener understands the entire picture and all its intricacies; they want the listener to get the full picture of what happened. Being process-oriented, women use the details of the full story to review the situation and draw a conclusion. Have you noticed how many women will discuss an issue in great detail, and then an hour later return to discuss the same situation in the same detail? Why? By talking about the situation she is processing the information and making decisions about her next steps. How does a man respond to this? "Do you have any new information? If not, I don't need to hear it." Or, "I thought we finished talking about this." "I thought you already made a decision."

Take the Message and Run: Mr. Fix-It

Men are focused on the task; they want to hear the facts in a quick and direct manner. Once they have the facts, then they can take action, complete the task, and move on. They are not interested in the emotions; emotions get in the way of the facts. Emotions can be distracting. Men get the information and may interrupt or stop listening when they have heard enough; they are ready to act on what they've heard.

While the man is focusing on completing the task, the woman is focusing on rethinking the information by talking about the situation again. She often would like the listener simply to acknowledge her concerns. She usually does not need the man to jump in and fix the situation. There are occasions when she will want the male listener to do something, in which case it is suggested that the woman tell him that is what's needed.

Exercise 5.4. Case Study: "Put Down That Smartphone and Listen to Me!"

Goal

Identify expected men's and women's listening behaviors.

Objectives

- Explore the men's and women's expectations for a "good" listener.

- Suggest what behaviors could have been done differently to improve the communication and listening between Janice and Malcolm.

Timing of Exercise

15 minutes total:

5 minutes to read the case and talk in small groups

10 minutes to hear the responses from each group or a sample of the groups

Materials

Handout: Case Study: "Put Down That Smartphone and Listen to Me!," chart paper and easel, markers

Optional: Create a slide to display the case study.

Setup

☐ Place the participants in coed groups of five to eight.

☐ Ask each group to assign a scribe who will take notes on the group's answers to the case study questions.

☐ The content for the handout includes the case study and questions. Distribute the handout and ask the participants to read it.

☐ Address each question with the entire class and ask for the individual group answers.

Case Study: "Put Down That Smartphone and Listen to Me!"

"Why doesn't he put down that smartphone and listen to me?" Janice sighed. "I know he can hear, but is he listening to me when he's scrolling madly on his phone?" she said, clearly frustrated at the situation. Her second issue: "Why isn't he looking at me when I talk to him? He seems distracted and more concerned about who is in the hallway."

Malcolm explains, "Janice, I am listening to you. I can do two things at once, you know. So what's the story on the new boss?" He continues scrolling.

"No, you're not. Put your phone down," Janice says.

"I hear every word you're saying," he replies, gazing at the group down the hallway.

"Okay. So what did I say?"

"You said something about a new boss from headquarters. Then you said why don't I put down my phone." Malcolm looks down as he intently texts on his phone.

Source: Copyright © 2012 by Audrey Nelson and Claire Damken Brown.

Questions

1. What happened?

2. List the behaviors of Janice and Malcolm that helped and those that hurt the discussion.

3. Was gender a concern in this communication? How?

4. How would you have managed the discussion?

5. What could both parties do to improve the situation?

Debrief

Sound familiar? The issues here are discovering why Janice doesn't think Malcolm is listening to her, and understanding why he doesn't put down his smartphone and look at her when she's speaking to him. Women often expect men to listen in the same manner women listen. Women are more attentive listeners. Women demonstrate many behaviors to show they are listening: nodding their head, leaning forward, uttering nonfluencies—short verbal expressions such as "Uh-huh"—or comments such as "That's right," looking at the speaker, and smiling at the speaker. Men tend not to look at the speaker. In fact, if you see two men speaking to each other, they are likely to be standing side by side, shoulder to shoulder, as they talk away. A woman expects the same nonverbal listening style that she employs. She's expecting him to put down his smartphone or report and look at her face as she talks about the new boss from headquarters. Meanwhile, the man may feel put upon since he thinks he was listening to her (and scrolling on his smartphone, too). This lack-of-listening scenario ends up with both parties feeling shortchanged.

Equally Able Listeners

Men and women are capable of listening—even to each other—and feeling good about being heard. While women are perceived as being better listeners due to their listening skills as mentioned above, men can learn these skills and also be perceived by women as having good listening skills. If men think it's tedious listening to women's details, men and women can learn how to be aware of the content they are sharing and phrase information to better suit the occasion.

Section 2: Women and Men Do Listen Differently

Exercise 5.5. How Women and Men Listen

Goal

Understand the verbal and nonverbal listening behaviors attributed to women and men.

Objectives

- Generate discussion and comments from the attendees about their experiences when speaking and listening to men and women.

- Create awareness of the impact on the workplace of gender differences in listening styles.

Timing of Exercise

20–30 minutes total:

8 to 10 minutes to complete the true/false questions and discuss them with the group

12–20 minutes to get comments from individuals or from a sample of the groups

Materials

Handout: How Women and Men Listen, chart paper and easel, markers

Setup

☐ Ask the participants to complete this true/false exercise individually or in a group. For example, the participants may complete the handout on their own and then form small coed groups of five to eight for discussion. Or you may initially form groups of five to eight members, in which members discuss and select their responses and then process them with the entire group.

☐ As an alternative, start by forming groups and assign each group particular questions that they will indicate as true or false and be responsible for discussing with the class.

☐ Ask the participants to indicate as true or false each item listed on the handout. If in small groups, ask the participants to discuss with the group members their reactions to the questions and reasoning for selecting true or false.

☐ At eight to ten minutes, get the group's attention and proceed with reviewing the true/false responses and discussion.

☐ Distribute the handout (Table 5.2).

Table 5.2. How Women and Men Listen

True/False	Read each item and mark as T (true) or F (false):
	1. Men listen for *feelings* as much as they listen for *facts*.
	2. If a person has something of a *personal nature* to share, they would prefer to share it with a man, rather than with a woman.
	3. Men tend to *stand indirectly*, rather than directly (face-to-face), and therefore are often perceived as not listening.
	4. Women tend to be *goal-oriented* in their listening style (listening for facts).
	5. Men often want to *fix or solve the problem* when they listen to a person's story.
	6. Women often incorporate many nonverbal behaviors (head nodding, leaning forward, facial expressions, and so on) into their communication, and are therefore often interpreted as *attentive* listeners.
	7. Men and women are *equally able listeners*.
	8. Women often want men to be more *understanding* when they listen.
	9. Women often include *details* in their speech that men perceive as unnecessary and, consequently, make it challenging for them to listen.
	10. Women tend to be *perceived* as better listeners than men.

Debrief

Use the following questions for group processing and discussion points:

1. Which questions did the participants have trouble deciding whether they were true or false? Why?

2. How did they come to that decision (true or false)?

3. Would they share an example that relates to the question or statement?

To reveal the correct true/false responses, you may choose to discuss each response one by one, asking for comments or thoughts on each question. Or you may reveal the correct true/false answers by displaying them on chart paper or on a slide and then asking for comments from the participants using the questions mentioned above. For a large group of forty or more or an auditorium-sized group, the facilitator may ask the audience for a show of hands indicating whether a question is true or false. Then after the last question, open it up for discussion and ask the audience if they have any comments on a particular question.

1. **False.** In general, men are listening for "facts" only. Men are considered goal-oriented; they want the facts so that they know how to react and can determine what action to take. Men are listening for content. They want to take action based on that content and fix the situation.

2. **False.** If a person has something of a personal nature to share, generally he or she would prefer to share it with a woman and not with a man. Both men and women agree that women are better listeners than men. What makes a better listener? Women's listening behaviors indicate that they are hearing and responding to the person speaking. Women nod their heads and utter "uh-huh" more often than men to show the speaker that they hear what the speaker is saying (but not necessarily agree with the speaker). Women do not interrupt as often as men; this is

another indicator that women are attentive and listening. Women also tend to show more empathy for the speaker, for example, commenting, "That must have been terrible for you" or "I'm glad to hear your son is feeling better. My nephew had that same surgery when he was seven."

3. **True.** Men tend to stand side by side or shoulder to shoulder when they speak with other men, and sometimes this behavior carries over to their conversations with women. Next time you're at a gathering, check out how the men position themselves when talking with each other. You will most likely see this side-by-side stance, as they converse indirectly (not face-to-face). Women tend to face the speaker so that they can better read the person's expressions in addition to the speaker's words. Because women are used to talking face-to-face, if a man uses the side-by-side stance, not looking at her face, she may very well think he's not listening to her.

4. **False.** Women are considered to be process-oriented (listening for feelings and facts), while men are considered to be goal-oriented (listening for the facts). Women hear the facts and the feelings and look at the relationships involved. They hear and discuss things more readily than men, including the feelings and emotions behind the facts. Women tend to talk more in a story format and may repeat information as they process it or come to terms with it and then make a decision. Men tend to hear the facts, take action or make a decision, and then are ready to move on to the next event or goal.

5. **True.** Men hear the facts and want to take action to resolve the situation as quickly as possible. Have you heard of Mr. Fix-It? Men tend to want to fix or solve the situation, check it off their list, and move on. When they listen to someone tell a story or talk about a problem, men generally are ready to jump in, interrupt, and offer one or more solutions.

6. **True.** Women's nonverbal responses, such as head nodding, leaning forward, facial expressions, and so on, are often

interpreted by the speaker as "attentive" listening. Note that these behaviors do not necessarily mean that she agrees with everything the speaker is saying.

7. **True.** Both men and women are quite capable of being good listeners. While women may say that their male colleagues don't listen to them, the men are adept at listening to six different sport broadcasts at once and relating the score in each game. When it comes to how well men and women listen to each other, it often depends on the situation and how the message is spoken.

8. **True.** Women do want men to be more "understanding" when they listen. But what does "understanding" mean? Women tend to want men to show the same listening behaviors that women use. For example, if men nodded their head, leaned forward, uttered "uh-huh" every once in a while, and did not interrupt, then women might interpret this as attentive listening or "understanding."

9. **True.** Women tend to be process-oriented, and part of that process is to understand how the details come together to describe a situation or form a story. It can be challenging for men to listen to women as they relate the details (often detail by detail by detail) describing a situation. Being task-oriented and more direct than women in their communication style, men tend to want the speaker to get to the point as quickly as possible so that they can fix it or take action and move on. Hearing all the details seems like extraneous information that's not needed for the man to take action. It becomes challenging for him as he listens to the details, not knowing which detail is most critical for him to take action. "Get to the bottom line" or "get to the point" is often a common lament from a man when listening to a woman relay her problem. He is hoping for a "yes or no" response. She is hoping for him to be attentive, even to empathize with her predicament, and to hear the whole situation before discussing any actions or next steps.

10. **True.** Women are perceived by both men and women as better listeners than men. Research shows that women do not interrupt the speaker as often as men do; this is perceived as respect for the speaker. Women tend to use nonverbal behaviors more frequently than men do in response to the speaker. This includes behaviors such as head nodding, facial expressions, nonfluencies or short verbal expressions ("uh-huh"), and comments ("I agree") to indicate that they are following what the speaker says. Women look face-to-face at the speaker more than men do; this is another indicator that is perceived as showing that women are better listeners.

training tip

Many exercises in this book may be completed individually or in a group. The facilitator needs to check their time and then decide what works best for the overall program and discussion time frame. With either choice, the facilitator can encourage a group discussion as part of the debrief. Individuals can volunteer their responses and thought processes; likewise, a small group's designated spokes-person can do the same.

Listening with the Eyes and Ears

Think about seeing the message. That's a woman's approach to listening. She hears and sees the message. She will usually stand looking at the speaker to better read the speaker's nonverbal behaviors. She's watching the speaker and adding to the message the speaker's vocal tones, gestures and body movement, and facial expressions. Women use this information to better understand and build a connection with the speaker. Men usually don't do this. Men orient themselves in a side-by-side stance and listen only to the words. When listening, men tend to not look directly at the speaker (Ivy & Backlund, 2004, p. 217).

Exercise 5.6. Listening: Men and Women Do It Differently

Goal

Examine the impact on conversation due to men's and women's listening behaviors.

Objectives

- Discuss women's and men's different listening behaviors in terms of the impact on the conversation.

- Discuss women's and men's different listening behaviors in terms of the conversation's meaning.

Timing of Exercise

15 minutes

Materials

Chart paper and easel, markers

Slide 5.4

Setup

☐ Ask the participants to work in dyads, with each person selecting someone sitting nearby.

☐ Ask the participants to view the slide and discuss the question at the end of the slide.

☐ Address the responses to the question with the entire class and ask for the individual group answers, time permitting.

> ## Slide 5.4
> ### LISTENING: Men and Women Do It Differently
>
> - Women generally read all of the speaker's behaviors that shape the message: gestures, facial expression, tone of voice, words, eye movement, touch, emotion, and more.
>
> - Men usually focus on the actual words or message.
>
> How do these behaviors affect the conversation's flow and meaning?
>
> ---
>
> *Source:* Copyright © 2012 by Audrey Nelson and Claire Damken Brown.

Debrief

In addition to being task-oriented, men tend to apply their listening behaviors in a self-oriented manner. Through the socialization of competitive skills, men learn to excel at speaking up for themselves and their needs. While listening, men use this self-orientation to look at how someone's message will affect them (Nelson, 2004, p. 258). In contrast, women hear the message in terms of the "other"; women tend to be other-oriented. When listening, women are thinking of how that message applies to their relationship with the speaker; women hear the words and feelings and want to support or help the speaker (C. Brown & Nelson, 2009, p. 56).

Issues happen between men and women when women assume men are hearing their complete message—and for women, that's words and feelings. Men assume they got the message, which was words only; they tend to miss the emotional and nonverbal layers of the message. While men are focusing on what action to take, women are looking at bonding and relationships. Women are relationship-oriented and, to a great extent, interpret what they hear in terms of how it affects the relationship. It's helpful for men to be aware that women will initiate conversations simply to establish or support the relationship and not because they need the men to do something (take action).

Women Listen Like the Split-Ear Mare

Women demonstrate a "split-ear phenomena," which is the same as the "split-ear mare" that has one ear aimed at her colt while another is aimed at the herd (Nelson, 2004, pp. 253–254; C. Brown & Nelson, 2009, p. 58). While the mare has its ears focusing on and listening to two different "audiences," her colt and the herd, women focus on and listen to different inputs, verbal and nonverbal. At one level with one ear she's listening to the words, and with the other ear or at the second level she's taking in all the nonverbal behaviors—such as vocal tone, facial expressions, and body movement—and using that information to further interpret the message that's conveyed. Men generally don't have this double-ear action happening; they are focused on the verbal part of the message.

Exercise 5.7. Listening: What Would You Like to Hear?

Goal

Examine men's and women's views of the listening behaviors they would like from each other.

Objectives

- Understand the listening behaviors women would like from men.

- Understand the listening behaviors men would like from women.

Timing of Exercise

15 minutes

Materials

Chart paper and easel, markers

Slide 5.5

Setup

☐ Ask the participants to work in dyads by selecting someone sitting nearby.

☐ Ask the participants to view the slide and discuss the questions.

☐ Address the responses to each question with the entire class and ask for the individual group answers, time permitting.

Slide 5.5

LISTENING: What Would You Like to Hear?

What are the reasons for the following?

1. Women want men to listen like women.

2. Men want women to listen like women.

3. Men and women believe that women are good listeners.

Source: Copyright © 2012 by Audrey Nelson and Claire Damken Brown.

Debrief

Women identified themselves as having a "relational, people-oriented style of listening" in a study by Johnston, Weaver, Watson, and Barker (2000, p. 32). They have a people-oriented style of listening, focused on the importance of emotions and feelings (p. 37). In contrast, men self-identified as having a more "action, content, and time-oriented style of listening" (p. 32). They have an action-oriented listening style focused on having exact information with no errors; a content style focused on receiving and assessing facts and complex information; and a time-oriented listening style focused on getting information quickly in short conversations (p. 37). Research by Sargent and Weaver (2003, p. 5) indicated that gender stereotypes influenced how men and women evaluate their peers' listening styles. Results indicated that women peers "were rated significantly higher on the people listening style measure than their" men peers. Peer men were viewed as having more of a "content listening style than peer women" (p. 13).

In *You Don't Say: Navigating Nonverbal Communication Between the Sexes*, Dr. Audrey Nelson discussed her research on men's and women's communication styles. Nelson indicated that women thought men were poor listeners and men agreed—they saw themselves as poor listeners. After asking more than one thousand people to indicate men's and women's communication strong and weak points, women also thought that men lack in showing emotions, cannot read nonverbal messages, take things too literally, and don't bother to listen or pretend to listen. Women thought that men interrupt and try to fix things (Nelson, 2004, pp. 20–23, 254–255).

In this same research, men thought that women overanalyze and apply too many emotions to things that are said. Women agreed that when listening they can be too empathetic. Overall men and women liked the way women listen. Men and women preferred women's listening style to that of men's listening style. Women's empathy (when not overdone), paraphrasing and reflecting, nonverbal messages (head nodding, facial expressions, and so on), facing the speaker, and not interrupting, all are positive indicators to the speaker that someone's listening (Nelson, 2004, pp. 20–23, 254–255).

Section 3: Improved Listening Skills for Women and Men

Recommended listening skills generally suggest that the listener look at the speaker; not interrupt; acknowledge the speaker with nonverbal behaviors, such as nodding your head or using short comments like "I see"; keep verbal and nonverbal responses consistent (for example, not smile when saying, "Sounds like you're upset"); and summarize or restate the speaker's message. Summarizing what the speaker says or the meaning of the message is described as *paraphrasing* (Tingley, 1994, p. 84). For example, the speaker comments, "I'm unable to get the report done this week since one of the team members is out. Fred is always out when I need him the most." A paraphrased reply might be, "It sounds like we'll need to move the due date since you're down a team member right now."

Another method of letting the speaker know you're listening is called *reflecting the message*: the listener captures the speaker's feelings and reflects them back. A reflective statement for the message above could be, "Sounds like it's frustrating for you when a team member you count on isn't there" (Tingley, 1994, p. 84). Reflecting a message's feelings is similar to women's style of listening: hearing content and emotions. It's a behavior that benefits both men and women to feel heard.

Men may turn off their listening when they ask a woman a question and get too long of a response in return. Men generally prefer short, direct responses so they can get the needed information, act on it, and continue on their way. When process- and relationship-oriented women respond to a man's "yes or no" question, they tend to share the whole story or process—who said what, who did what, when it all happened, who was there, what they were wearing, and so on—and then get to the "yes or no" part. Meanwhile the man is waiting to get the information he wants so that he can solve the problem (he's task-oriented). He may have already interrupted the woman with "Get to the point," "Is it a yes or no?" or "I don't know how any of this relates to my question." He's frustrated and thinks she's avoiding his question. She's frustrated and feels he is rude for interrupting her; she thinks he doesn't want to hear all that she has to say. This is a signal to her that he's clearly not interested in maintaining a work relationship.

To help avoid these frustrations, we suggest that women respond using sound bites. The man asks a question, and the woman responds briefly in one or two words (like a short sound bite). If he needs more information, he'll ask and then she can respond in another sound bite of a few words. If he still needs more details, she can then provide more information, or ask, "How much detail do you want—just the highlights or the nitty-gritty?" This can also be described as responding by using a bulleted list with short, crisp points. The man asks a question and the woman responds with the first bullet. He asks for more information and she provides the next bullet. For example, he asks, "Can you get the statistics to me for Wednesday's meeting?" She uses the sound bite or bullet style and says, "I will have the numbers to you by noon." She does not use the longer, process-oriented version: "I have a conference call with headquarters and will need to ask Yolanda to run these numbers. That is, if I can catch up with her. She has been hard to find since she has been assigned to the project. But I should be able to get those numbers to you by noon." Nelson (2004, p. 257) refers to this response style as the pyramid style. When a man asks a question, a woman responds with one word—the top of the pyramid. If the man needs more information, he'll ask, and she responds with a few more words—the middle of the pyramid. And if he still needs more information, she replies with all the details that form the base of the pyramid (C. Brown & Nelson, 2009, p. 38).

Slide 5.6

Women's Responses Use Sound-Bite or Bullet Style

Say this: I will have the numbers to you by noon.

Don't say this: I have a conference call with headquarters and will need to ask Yolanda to run these numbers. That is, if I can catch up with her. She has been hard to find since she has been assigned to the project. But I should be able to get those numbers to you by noon.

Source: Copyright © 2012 by Audrey Nelson and Claire Damken Brown.

Once men are aware that women tend to share more of the process and details of what happened, then men may choose to phrase their questions in the following manner: "This is a quick yes or no. Have you received the data for Thursday's report?" Or, "I need some quick information now, and you can fill me in on the details later." With both men and women improving their listening skills, better communication is ready to happen.

Exercise 5.8. Case Study: Listening for the Process and Details

Goal

Identify the steps to take when men think women provide "too much detail."

Objectives

- Explore how a man's and woman's perspectives on listening differ during a specific conversation.

- Begin to look at what behaviors could have been done differently to improve the communication and listening between Jack and Sally.

- Review the short, direct bullet-style of communicating and how it would benefit Sally and Jack's conversation.

Timing of Exercise

20 minutes total:

8 minutes to read the case and talk in small groups

12 minutes to hear the responses from each group or from a sample of groups

Materials

Handout: Case Study: "Get to the Point!," chart paper and easel, markers

Optional: Create a slide to display the case study.

Setup

☐ Place participants in coed groups of five to eight.

☐ The content for the handout includes the case study and questions. Distribute the handout and ask the participants to read it.

☐ Ask each group to assign a scribe who will take notes on the group's answers to the case study questions.

☐ Address each question with the entire class and ask for the individual group answers.

training tip

To keep the discussions moving, the facilitator may assign particular questions in the exercise to different small groups, letting them know that they will be responsible for discussing their responses to those questions with the larger group.

Case Study: "Get to the Point!"

"Jack, you're not listening to me!" exclaimed Sally. They sat at their usual Thursday project meeting with the team reviewing the status of the group's activities.

"Sally, get to the point," replied Jack.

"I was getting to the point if you would just let me finish." Clearly upset, Sally continued, "I told you Bob was out this week. His wife is having surgery, and he's home taking care of the kids. I'm really worried about how his wife is doing. It's quite serious. I did not get access to his data until early this morning, so it still needs to be reviewed by Joan before it's formatted for the report. Joan, did you receive my e-mail with the data?"

Sitting up in his chair, Jack leaned forward and sternly said, "Look, do you have the report or not?" Joan glanced over at Sally. Sally's face and neck turned bright red.

"That's what I've been trying to tell you for the past ten minutes if you would only listen," Sally's voice cracked as she answered Jack's question. The other team members looked uncomfortable. Bill and Frank kept their eyes glued to their laptops and acted as if they didn't hear anything. Joan looked down and shuffled the papers on the table in front of her.

Jack rolled his eyes, breathed a heavy sigh, and said, "Here we go again."

Source: Copyright © 2012 by Audrey Nelson and Claire Damken Brown.

Questions

1. What happened?

2. List the behaviors of Jack and Sally that helped and that hurt the discussion.

3. Was gender a concern in this communication? How?

4. How would you have managed the discussion?

5. What could both parties do to improve the situation?

6. How could both parties stop this from happening again?

Debrief

Jack's heavy sigh, eye rolling, and commenting to the group, "Here we go again," indicate Jack's frustration with a situation that's happened before. Jack and Sally need to be specific about their expectations in this workplace conversation. By stating, "This is a yes or no question. You can fill me in on the details later," Jack could eliminate his own frustration at listening and not getting the answer he needs. Jane could do something similar by telling Jack she has more information about what's delaying the report and then schedule time to talk about it outside the group meeting. The case doesn't say if Jack or Sally is the boss, but it is always good form to let the boss or colleague know as early as possible that there's a delay or that a particular project date will not be met.

It would help the business relationship and conversation for Jack to hear and acknowledge that Sally is upset and concerned for Bob and his wife and that she's frustrated with Jack's impatience as she explains the delay. For example, Jack could use reflective listening by replying, "Sounds like you're concerned about Bob and his family. Perhaps we could talk about it after the meeting." Or he could say, "It sounds like this delay is frustrating for you." In this manner, Sally would feel that Jack is listening to her and not solely focused on his task of getting the status of the final report.

Sally could help the situation by using the "precue" method of letting Jack know what type of reply she'd like. She could say, "I need you to listen for a moment about how frustrating this delay has been for me and the team. I don't need you to do anything right now. I have it in check." Then if the topic is appropriate for the team meeting, she could say she's concerned about Bob's family, she now has the data, and Joan is reviewing it. If Sally needs Jack's assistance, she could respond directly, "I'm concerned that Bob is out, and I could use some suggestions to get the data finalized quickly for the report." Then Jack and the team could spend a few minutes talking about how to get the report finished.

Women, take charge of what you need
and cue the man.

To help get a man out of the fix-it mode, a woman can "precue" him before the conversation. In advance of the conversation, she can take a moment to think about what she's expecting or wanting him to do with the information she provides. This will help him listen for what it is she wants. She will feel supported; he has heard her request and message. What is she expecting? If she's looking for him to listen and acknowledge her comments, she can state, "I need to vent and would like you to listen; no action is needed." If she's looking for information, tell him, "You've done this work before; I'd like to hear your suggestions." If she needs action, she could say, "I'd like your help to solve this." This information up front will help the man know what the woman needs and respond appropriately. The woman will feel that he's listening. (See slide 5.7.)

Slide 5.7

WOMEN: Tell Him What You Need

Cue him:

- You need him to act.

- You want to unload or vent.

- This is an FYI (For Your Information) only.

- You would like an affirmation or acknowledgment.

Source: Copyright © 2012 by Audrey Nelson and Claire Damken Brown.

Slide 5.8

MEN AND WOMEN: Decide to Be
Effective Listeners

Effective listening:

- Takes time and effort.

- Requires a decision to listen.

- Benefits from an appointment: schedule time to meet and listen to each other.

- Takes practice: model your new listening skills at the office.

Source: Copyright © 2012 by Audrey Nelson and Claire Damken Brown.

Use the Action Steps slides (on pages 169 and 170) for men and women as part of your summary for the material you presented from this chapter.

Slide 5.9

Action Steps for Men

When listening to women . . .

- Use paraphrasing in your response.

- Listen for feelings. Reflect back the emotions you hear.

- Tell her if you need a quick response or a "yes or no."

- Use more nonverbal behaviors to show that you're listening (nod your head, lean forward, look at the speaker).

- Face the speaker.

- Incorporate nonfluencies such as "uh-huh," "gee," and one- or two-word responses such as "I agree," "Yeah," or "That works."

- Do not interrupt.

- Realize that you are not responsible for fixing and solving her problems. Ask, "How can I support you?" or "Is there anything you want me to do?"

Source: Copyright © 2012 by Audrey Nelson and Claire Damken Brown.

Slide 5.10

Action Steps for Women

When listening to men . . .

- Use paraphrasing in your response.

- Talk in sound bites.

- Use the "pyramid" or bullet style of brief responses.

- Let him know you will share more details if asked.

- Be direct in your responses.

- Cue him when you share a concern. Some possible choices could be: (1) you need him to act; (2) you want to unload or vent; (3) it is an FYI (For Your Information); and (4) you would like an affirmation or acknowledgment.

- Do not get derailed by overanalyzing the feelings or emotions you think you hear. Reflect back a message to confirm that the emotions you hear are accurate.

Source: Copyright © 2012 by Audrey Nelson and Claire Damken Brown.

CHAPTER 6

Men, Women, and Conflict

Take It Like a Man Versus Nice Girls Don't Do Conflict

> *The Chinese have a character for conflict that consists of two symbols: one for* opportunity *and the other for* danger.
>
> —*Victor H. Mair (2009)*

Learning Objectives

- Understand and self-assess how gender-conflict styles are developmentally formed and evolve to shape adult conflict-management repertoires.

- Determine how women's conflict mantra, "Harmony is normal and conflict is abnormal," affects conflict outcomes.

- Know how men's conflict mantra, "Winning at any cost is the name of the game," affects conflict outcomes.

171

- Distinguish the double standard of how men and women express anger with a *flight* or *fight* approach.

- Analyze how women show vulnerability and men manifest control in conflict situations.

- Suggest action steps for women and men to manage conflict more productively.

Introduction

We know conflict is inevitable. It is a natural, normal part of life. Where there are relationships, there will be conflict. A critical component of successful male-female relationships is the ability of the couple or coworkers to handle conflict, whether it is in the boardroom or the bedroom. In fact, handling conflict, or not handling conflict, is often considered one of the explanations for the fifty-fifty survival rate of marriages. The workplace is equally riddled with poorly managed conflicts affecting the bottom line.

No workplace is without conflict. When men and women are not equipped with productive conflict-management tools and a comprehension of sex differences, it can result in problems that are costly, such as retention, low morale, and poorly functioning teams. Women and men can learn more productive responses and help each other resolve their disputes.

Timing for Unit

1 hour and 45 minutes to 2 hours

Materials for Unit

Handouts, chart paper and easel, markers
Slides 6.1 through 6.17

Section 1: The Playground as Battleground

Exercise 6.1. Self-Assessment of Childhood Conflict Patterns

Goal

Identify common sex-role themes played out by women and men in conflict.

Objectives

- Identify the common childhood sex-role expectations and how they develop.

- Explore and identify how sex-role norms influence adult conflict-management styles.

Timing of Exercise

15–20 minutes

Materials

Handout: Warm-Up Exercise: The Playground as Battleground, chart paper and easel, markers

Slide 6.1

Setup

☐ Conduct this exercise in dyads and then process the results with the entire group, or conduct it in groups of five to eight members, in which each member shares his or her response, and then process the responses with the entire group.

☐ The content for the handout is the same as the content on the slide. Distribute the handout.

Slide 6.1

WARM-UP EXERCISE: The Playground as Battleground

Select the statements that apply to your childhood experience. Mark "F" for the items that you perceive are more characteristically female styles and "M" for the items that you perceive are more characteristically male styles:

1. ___ I played cooperatively and wanted to make sure everyone was included.

2. ___ I played with others by teasing, shoving, pushing, and bantering.

3. ___ I took care of others.

4. ___ I liked taking classmates on and challenging their ideas.

5. ___ I worked for everyone to get along.

6. ___ I ignored and excluded classmates when they hurt my feelings.

7. ___ I told classmates when I was mad at them.

8. ___ I would take a backseat to others.

9. ___ I wanted to be heard when I did not like something.

10. List a way that you handled conflict with your classmates. Do you think it was gender linked?

Source: Copyright © 2012 by Audrey Nelson and Claire Damken Brown.

Debrief

In the warm-up exercise, the styles depicted in the statements tend to be characteristically:

1. **Female.** Girls tend to play cooperatively, negotiating relationships to ensure that everyone is included and has a role. Playing "nice" is the goal. A *Wall Street Journal* article talked about awards given to five-year-old kindergarten students in the Midwest. The awards designated for the girls were "Biggest Heart," "Best Helper," and "All-Around Sweetheart" (Deveny, 1994, p. B1).

2. **Male.** In contrast, boys play rougher and louder (ask any elementary school teacher). Boys are more physical.

3. **Female.** At a very young age, girls exhibit caretaking behaviors. If someone falls and gets hurt, the girls will gather around that person to soothe and comfort them. Social maintenance will be shared among girls, taking care not to hurt feelings or leave anyone out of a game.

4. **Male.** Boys learn to connect through play banter. Challenging each other is the game boys play out daily on the playground and in the classroom. Boys begin to compete with each other in every arena. Play fighting and challenging is where competitive skills begin to form.

5. **Female.** Girls are rewarded for social skills, such as getting along well with others and not making waves. Being agreeable, avoiding confrontation, and helping the group cooperate are the goals for girls.

6. **Female.** When girls get upset with others, they will use social currency as retribution. Ostracizing and excluding others is one of the most common practices among girls.

7. **Male.** Boys tend to express dissatisfaction and conflict directly. You will hear boys say, "I don't like you" or "Don't do that." It may also be accompanied by a push or shove.

8. **Female.** Girls will more often acquiesce to others rather than challenge an emerging leader. There is an "alpha" girl type who exhibits dominance, and other girls will quickly defer to her.

9. **Male.** Often the more a boy objects to something, the louder he becomes. It is common for boys to display dissatisfaction by loud outbursts such as "No," "Leave me alone," or "Stop that."

And in response to the last question:

10. Have the group share their personal childhood experiences handling conflict and encourage them to share stories that illustrate gender differences.

Slide 6.2

Boys and Bantering Versus Girls and Relational Methods of Fighting

Boys and girls are raised to have different beliefs and views about conflict and what it means to "win" a conflict.

Source: Copyright © 2012 by Audrey Nelson and Claire Damken Brown.

From the playground to the boardroom, boys and girls learn different methods for handling conflict. Your membership in a gender group is formed early, remains for a lifetime, and is one of the most influential and powerful determining factors in developing your conflict-management repertoire.

Traditionally, girls are taught to be noncompetitive, nonaggressive, compliant, and interdependent. Girls put relationships first and winning second; boys learn how to compete early in life, and the expectation is to be dominant, strong, and independent. Boys and girls are raised to have different beliefs and views about conflict and what it means to "win" a conflict.

Girls and women put a premium on not rocking the boat, getting along, and trying to keep the peace. For women, interdependence forms the root of their way of handling conflicts. Relationships and connections to others are paramount. In addition, it is not considered feminine to be engaged in conflict. Nice girls don't do conflict. A girl often will become a "people pleaser" and adopt accommodation and avoidance as conflict styles. She will say "yes" when she really wants to say "no." In contrast, men often perceive "no" as "go." No becomes a challenge, something to conquer.

Young children demonstrate sex-linked differences in negotiating and managing conflict early in their development. Girls from ages five to seven will employ communication strategies that diffuse or de-escalate conflict; in contrast, boys will engage in heavy-handed tactics before they resort to trying less confrontational means of resolution.

A study conducted at Purdue University by child-development experts Laura Hess and Marc Atkins (1998) shows that a marked sex difference exists as early as elementary school when it comes to styles of handling conflict. Hess claimed, "Woe to the girl who is overly aggressive" (p. 86). Her research shows that girls who are disruptive and aggressive are at a much greater risk of being rejected by their peers than are their male counterparts. A rejection from peers is a high price to pay for girls who place a high value on relationship and connection.

Girls generally play cooperatively in groups. Boys organize themselves into *hierarchical* groups more than girls do, with one designated leader. The rest of the boys are left to jockey for second and third positions by acting tough and aggressive. Girls experience *flat organizations* rather than hierarchical ones. The premium is on getting along with others and learning how to negotiate and smooth over differences to save and preserve friendships. Girls prefer reciprocity and intimacy in playing games. These lessons have served women

Slide 6.3

Social Organizations of Boys Versus Girls

Boys = hierarchical organization

Girls = flat organization

Source: Copyright © 2012 by Audrey Nelson and Claire Damken Brown.

well in terms of developing interpersonal competency, enhanced social skills, and the ability to sustain relationships. In contrast, boys learn that relationship maintenance is secondary, and consequently resort more to winning, playing tough, competitiveness, and aggressiveness. For boys, competition is the name of the game. Winning at all costs is the motto; whatever it takes, including hurting other people's feelings for the sake of being on top. For boys and men, competition is like a sport. Like a game, it is fun to strategize on how to win and the process is invigorating. The male agenda is to crush the opposition.

> Boys organize into hierarchical groups and girls in flat organizations.

Boys also learn to be friends with their opponents. The kinds of childhood games that boys play are competitive and combative. If boys did not become friends with their enemies, they would have no friends. Boys learn to separate play from their friendships.

In contrast to the cooperative play among girls, you have the rough-and-tumble world of boys. Drive by a playground and watch boys rip the hat off the head of their buddy or steal his lunch and run with it, hoping to be chased. Boys and men challenge each other; they enjoy an adversarial stance. From childhood to adulthood, men are taught to be aggressive, competitive, and independent. Men may actually score notches on their belt for standing alone on an issue. Men are interested in power: how to get it and use it. It is not uncommon to see men engage in a sort of play fighting or bantering during the Monday morning staff meetings. Lobbing insults and challenging their male coworkers to beat their sales figures is a regular formula that is interpreted as male bonding. Linguist Deborah Tannen (1994) suggests that banter is a form of "verbal mock attack." Through fighting men connect. A male motto might be: *If I care enough about you, I will "fight" with you.*

Boys and men learn to be friends with
their opponents.

Girls and women are caught off guard and don't know what to do when boys and men banter. Many women become paralyzed by and anxious around the interaction, take the banter literally, and misread it for a "real" fight. Women seldom banter. It is almost nonexistent in female culture and can often cause moments of discomfort for women when men engage in this predictable ritual.

Girls and women are caught off guard
by male banter.

Exercise 6.2. Reflection Exercise for Women

Goal

Identify common sex-role themes played out by women in conflict.

Objectives

- Identify feminine themes and sex-role prescriptions.

- Understand how these sex-role prescriptions are manifested in conflict.

Timing of Exercise

15–20 minutes

Materials

Handout: Do Women in the Group Resonate with Any of These Themes?, chart paper and easel, markers

Slides 6.4 and 6.5

Setup

☐ Break into coed groups.

☐ Ask the groups to nominate a scribe who will jot down notes on three major points made by the group to share with the entire group.

☐ Women will lead the exercise, and men will join in by asking questions and offering comments about how this kind of approach to conflict could impact decision making and resolving conflict in the workplace.

☐ Distribute the handout.

Slide 6.4

Women's Conflict Mantra

Harmony is normal and conflict is abnormal.

Source: Copyright © 2012 by Audrey Nelson and Claire Damken Brown.

Slide 6.5

Reflection for Women

Do any of these sayings resonate with you?

Taking care of others

Taking a backseat

Acting dumb

Being the power behind the throne

Suffering silently

Playing nice

Waiting to be saved

Being seen, not heard

Sacrificing yourself for others

Being a people pleaser

Not rocking the boat

Keeping and making the peace

Source: Copyright © 2012 by Audrey Nelson and Claire Damken Brown.

Sample Handout Text: Do Women in the Group Resonate with Any of These Themes?

- Taking care of others: "I like playing 'office mom' when people seek me out with their troubles."

- Taking a backseat: "I don't need to express my opinion with such a strong group."

- Acting dumb: "I can't express my expertise on this issue."

- Being the power behind the throne: "It's okay if I don't get the acknowledgment for the work I do behind the scenes for my manager."

- Suffering silently: "That was inappropriate, but I will remain quiet about it."

- Playing nice: "If I act nice to my coworkers, no one will confront me."

- Waiting to be saved: "My supervisor will intervene on my behalf."

- Being seen, not heard: "I don't speak up in meetings."

- Sacrificing yourself for others: "It's okay if I did not get the credit I deserve. She needs it more."

- Being a people pleaser: "My need to have people like me is stronger than voicing my true opinion."

- Not rocking the boat: "I don't want to be a troublemaker."

- Keeping and making the peace: "My need to have everyone get along is more important than addressing this issue."

Debrief

Every group gets a turn to share three major points made about the underlying principles that guide women's conflict style.

Here are the facilitator questions for group processing and discussion points:

1. What implication does this have for handling everyday conflict at work (financial costs, lack of promotion and career progress, acting out resentment in indirect ways such as passive-aggressive behavior, and inferior decision making)?

2. What are some methods of communication that could be employed to counteract these potentially dysfunctional styles?

   - Draw women into controversy: "Ginny, every proposal has its strengths and weaknesses. Can you share a weakness?"

   - Let her know it is okay to "agree to disagree": "Let's not fall into groupthink."

   - Create a culture where it is okay to express a different opinion and still remain collegial, especially for women. A disagreement does not have to result in making enemies.

   - Set the rules of engagement to include the full participation of everyone. Don't allow one person to dominate and take all the airtime.

   - What new thoughts and insights has the group gained about how women handle conflict?

Exercise 6.3. Reflection Exercise for Men

Goal

Identify common sex-role themes played out by men in conflict.

Objectives

- Identify masculine themes and sex-role prescriptions.

- Understand how these prescriptions are manifested in conflict.

- Gain personal awareness of the messages that underlie men's conflict style.

Timing of Exercise

15–20 minutes

Materials

Handout: Do the Men in the Group Resonate with Any of These Themes?, chart paper and easel, markers

Slides 6.6 and 6.7

Setup

☐ Break into coed groups and distribute the handout.

☐ Ask each group to nominate a scribe who will jot down notes on three major points made by the group to share with the entire group.

☐ Men lead this exercise, and women join in by asking questions and offering comments about how this kind of approach to conflict could affect decision making and resolving conflict in the workplace.

Slide 6.6

Men's Conflict Mantra

Winning at any cost is the name of the game.

Source: Copyright © 2012 by Audrey Nelson and Claire Damken Brown.

Slide 6.7

Reflection for Men

Do any of these sayings resonate with you?

Competition is the name of the game.

I will use power plays.

Winning is all that matters.

I can step up to the plate.

Playing games is okay in conflict.

Sometimes you break the rules.

Not everyone has to be my best friend.

I don't want to take a backseat to anyone.

Conflict is risky, and I will take that chance.

I can take criticism and accusations in a conflict.

I have no problem saying "No" to demands in a conflict.

I stay focused on the goal.

Source: Copyright © 2012 by Audrey Nelson and Claire Damken Brown.

Sample Handout Text: Do the Men in the Group Resonate with Any of These Themes?

• Competition is the name of the game: "I will do whatever it takes to win."

• I will use power plays: "It is important that I look like a formidable player."

• Winning is all that matters: "It's not if you win or lose, it is how you play the game."

- I can step up to the plate: "I can take whatever they throw at me."

- Playing games is okay in conflict: "Playing it safe won't always get you what you want."

- Sometimes you break the rules: "I know rules are made to be broken."

- Not everyone has to be my best friend: "It's okay if people get irritated with me. I am not here for a popularity contest."

- I don't want to take a backseat to anyone: "Being front and center stage is important for recognition and getting ahead."

- Conflict is risky, and I will take that chance: "Risk taking is exhilarating and fun."

- I can take criticism and accusations in a conflict: "I don't take criticism personally, and even if it bothers me, I will never let on."

- I have no problem saying "no" to demands in a conflict: "I can set boundaries."

- I stay focused on the goal: "I always have my eye on the end result, and how I get there isn't that important."

Debrief

Every group gets a turn to share three major points made about the underlying principles that guide men's conflict style.

Here are the facilitator questions for group processing and discussion points:

1. What implication does this have for handling everyday conflict at work (financial costs, lack of promotion and career progress, and inferior decision making)?

2. What are some methods of communication that could be employed to counteract these potentially dysfunctional styles?

   - Suggest incorporating "rapport" talk in conflict, addressing both the issue and people's feelings about the issue. Try to build relationships: "I care about our relationship, and I know we can work this out."

- Add more emotional content and explanation. Men often reflect a more "competitive" interaction style to resolve conflicts. This includes increased interrupting, overlapping (talking over someone and usually louder), and providing more succinct information with less emotional content. Women will typically respond better to more emotional content and, if warranted, a longer explanation.

- Set guidelines for transparency and minimize game playing: "I will tell you how I really feel about things."

- Emphasize that the "process" is equally as important as the goal.

3. What new thoughts and insights has the group gained about how men handle conflict?

training tip

This chapter builds on past discussions that examined how boys and girls are socialized and learn "appropriate" male and female communication roles. The chapter may be combined with Chapter Two, "He Speaks, She Speaks." Use the discussions from earlier in the book to look at how gender socialization affects adults' approaches, while discussing gender communication's impact on managing conflict. For example, an analysis of Deborah Tannen's linguistic gender differences in *You Just Don't Understand* (1990) provides insights and implications for tactics employed by women and men in conflict. The following is a summary of the linguistic style differences discussed in Chapter Two that can be exhibited in a conflict:

Female	Male
Connection	Competition
Support	Challenge
Understanding	Advice
Feeling	Solution
Egalitarian	Hierarchical
Cooperation	Authority
Comply	Defy

Section 2: Nice Girls Don't Do Conflict

Exercise 6.4. Case Study:
Nice Girls Don't Do Conflict

Goal

Identify how women present double messages and the impact on conflict management.

Objectives

- Understand how contradictions between verbal and nonverbal messages affect conflict and women's credibility.

- Analyze alternative responses to sending double messages.

Timing of Exercise

15–20 minutes

Materials

Handout: Case Study: Nice Girls Don't Do Conflict, chart paper and easel, markers

Setup

☐ Place the participants in coed groups of five to eight.

☐ Ask each group to assign a scribe who will take notes on the group's answers to the questions.

☐ The content for the handout includes the case study and questions. Distribute the handout and ask the participants to read it.

☐ Address each question with the entire class and ask for the individual group answers.

Case Study: Nice Girls Don't Do Conflict

Take the case of Karen, the thirty-two-year-old director of advertising at a midsized apparel company. I observed her and her team when I consulted at one of their monthly staff meetings. When it was Karen's turn to speak, the vice president of her division turned to her and asked, "How are you doing?"

"Not all that well," she replied gravely. "It took six months for me to finally get my raise—the one that was retroactive to January 1. I couldn't believe how much bureaucratic garbage I had to go through." As she shared the gory details, the rest of the staff nodded supportively.

"That's awful," one of her colleagues said.

"What a pain," chimed in another.

Even the vice president was taken aback. "They should never have put you through all that," he said, shaking his head.

Then, just as Karen was about to finish her tale of woe, she flashed a quick smile. As if on cue, the men in the room shifted uncomfortably in their chairs. They looked perplexed.

Source: Copyright © 2012 by Audrey Nelson and Claire Damken Brown.

Questions

1. What did that smile mean? Was Karen really as upset as she said she was?

2. Could they take her complaints seriously?

3. Is her credibility jeopardized? How and why?

4. Would the vice president feel compelled to follow up on her grievance, now that she seemed to discount it so handily?

5. What could Karen have done differently?

Debrief

Karen's face contradicted her words. Indeed, that seemingly innocuous smile undermined her compelling verbal expressions of frustration and distress. No wonder her male colleagues seemed puzzled; Karen had shot herself in the foot with her female nonverbal style. Unfortunately, women often subvert their own credibility by these kinds of conflicting messages. And Karen's obvious lack of consciousness about what she had just done would most likely come back to haunt her later in her career.

Karen did what a lot of women do in conflict: they send conflicting messages, saying one thing and doing something else nonverbally. This is confusing and sends mixed messages, eroding women's credibility. Women often use nonverbal signals, especially the smile, to soften the blunt force of a conflict. She cannot jeopardize her femininity, and she feels the need to get over her anger as if she has the flu. Women are not supposed to rock the boat; they are supposed to be master negotiators and serve as peacemakers.

> Women often send conflicting messages, saying one thing and doing something else nonverbally.

Section 3: Play Fighting

Exercise 6.5. Case Study: The Male Banter Game

Goal

Create an awareness of how men use bantering and play devil's advocate.

Objectives

- Understand the purpose of male bantering.

- Analyze how men and women have different reactions to male bantering.

- Identify ways that male bantering could exclude women.

Timing of Exercise

15–20 minutes

Materials

Handout: Case Study: The Male Banter Game, chart paper and easel, markers

Slide 6.8

Setup

☐ Place participants in coed groups of five to eight.

☐ Ask each group to assign a scribe who will takes notes on the group's answers to the questions.

☐ The content for the handout includes the case study and questions. Distribute the handout and ask the participants to read it.

☐ Address each question with the entire class and ask for the individual group answers.

Slide 6.8

PLAY FIGHTING: The Male Banter Game

Source: Copyright © 2012 by Audrey Nelson and Claire Damken Brown.

Case Study: The Male Banter Game

Roger was a mid-level manager at a technology company and enjoyed teasing, joking, and bantering with his coworkers. Some of his coworkers claimed it was a "sport" for him, never intended to hurt feelings but to get his colleagues to have a little fun and incorporate some play fighting at work. The Monday morning staff meeting usually began with Roger's ritual insults and digs. All of his colleagues waited for him to get going on the sparring. Usually the bantering was exchanged between Roger and his male coworkers, who seemed to engage and give it right back to him. The women were simply spectators. But one morning Roger threw a challenge to Ginny, who had the lead on a new tech project. In a playful tone, Roger said, "Hey Ginny, how in the world are you ever going to make these deadlines? You are going to have to become 'Ginny the Genie' to make that happen." Roger had the highest respect for Ginny, and she was known by all to be one of the most valued members on the team. Roger meant no harm, but because of Ginny's established position felt that she was "fair game" for sparring. Unfortunately, Ginny looked visibly ruffled and later disclosed that her feelings were hurt by Roger's "lack of respect for her ability to get the deadlines met."

Source: Copyright © 2012 by Audrey Nelson and Claire Damken Brown.

Questions

1. Does Roger's bantering set the tone for the meeting? In what way?

2. Because bantering is usually exchanged between men, are women at risk of being left out of the opportunity to bond with male team members?

3. How could Ginny have responded differently to Roger's bantering?

4. Do you think the team could perceive Ginny as "thin-skinned"?

5. Does anyone engage in bantering at your workplace?

6. What could Roger have done differently?

Debrief

Men enjoy and appreciate an adversarial stance. It is a way of connecting and a form of a compliment: "You care enough to fight with me." They see challenge as a way of honoring someone's knowledge or position. Roger was honoring Ginny by challenging her. Men like to play the devil's advocate. They like to take someone's idea and rip it apart and turn it upside down. Men never get over ritual combat. Women would prefer for everyone to play nicely, and they want everyone to agree in a discussion. Look around the room the next time a heated debate begins; you'll observe the women getting uncomfortable. We have seen women excuse themselves from a meeting when things got too hot. Conflict can intensify when women perceive men's bantering and playing the devil's advocate as real conflict, not the reverence men intend. For men, it is often a form of flattery if they engage you in opposition.

Men enjoy play fighting or bantering.

The next time a man is bantering or play fighting and you're thinking, "This is war," remember that it's only a little rumble. Men generally enjoy the process more than women. That's motivation for women to get over it quickly. Men often turn business into a game, and they want to spar with their opponents. This isn't an emotional crisis or personal attack, just a little fun. It's sport.

Section 4: The Anger Advantage

Exercise 6.6. Flight or Fight?

Goal

Identify the role gender plays in expressing anger in conflict.

Objectives

- Explore how sex roles affect the expression of anger in conflict.

- Understand how women's styles, such as avoidance, accommodation, and passive-aggressive behavior, can result in dysfunctional conflict.

- Understand how men's styles, such as competition, aggressive anger, and not addressing the feelings or emotions, can result in dysfunctional conflict.

Timing of Exercise

15–20 minutes

Materials

Handout: Reflection for Women, chart paper and easel, markers

Slide 6.9

Setup

☐ Place the participants in coed groups of five to eight.

☐ Ask the women in the group to respond to the sayings in the handout.

☐ Distribute the handout.

Slide 6.9

THE ANGER ADVANTAGE: Flight or Fight?

Source: Copyright © 2012 by Audrey Nelson and Claire Damken Brown.

Sample Handout Text: Reflection for Women

Do any of these sayings resonate with you?

- Time will take care of it.

- It isn't nice to get angry.

- It's no big deal.

- Don't sweat the small stuff.

- I shouldn't have angry thoughts.

- I will just keep it to myself.

- I should just forget about it.

- If you can't say something nice, don't say anything at all.

Debrief

All these themes can be sophisticated forms of avoidance. It is true that it is important for time and stress management to accurately identify what battles are worth fighting, but when no battles are fought, that may be a red flag for avoidance.

Psychological research tells us that women have higher rates of depression than men. The operational definition of depression is anger turned inward. Women suppress their anger, and men express it. A woman can take the anger out on herself by beating herself up with guilt, depression, self-sabotage, and self-doubt.

Anger is a normal and natural response with deep evolutionary roots that has evolved to help us cope with the violation of boundaries, frustration, hurt, and threats. Anger is life affirming; it calls for change. Anger is a signal that something is wrong and is often a part of conflict. To maintain any self-integrity, it is important that we address our anger. It is also a *secondary* emotion rather than a primary emotion. Underneath anger is usually the fear of unmet needs. Anger is vital to conflict situations. How we deal with anger in a conflict will often determine whether the conflict is productive or destructive.

The expression of anger is also gender-marked. For men, it is generally acceptable to express anger. In fact, it is often the one sanctioned emotion men can express publicly. The man is perceived as "taking a stand" and setting boundaries, the ultimate expression of masculinity. Our culture shapes this male response, and it may be an extension of the male role as "protector." It is his opportunity to demonstrate courage and prove his self-worth. It is the survival of the fittest. And he will hold his ground and not back down. He will choose to *fight* and meet the opponent head on; taking *flight* is not an option.

He will choose *fight*, and she will choose *flight*.

In conflict, women who openly express anger at men are especially suspect. Men in return often feel more threatened when confronted by a woman; they expect to be taken on by their own gender, not by women. The violation of prescribed gender roles when a woman openly challenges a man presents a possible risk to his sex role. Consequently, a man may fight harder with a woman than with another man to win his point and deflect her anger. Just the act of directly expressing anger, especially at men, makes a woman appear unladylike, unfeminine, and unmaternal. Remember, a woman's role is to care for others, both at home and work.

For women, anger is not perceived as synonymous or congruent with femininity. Women should not express strong feelings such as anger. In *The Princessa: Machiavelli for Women* (1998), Harriet Rubin claims that "when the tension is overwhelming, women often withdraw, or react in anger, then regret the outburst" (p. 68). Women try to get over anger like the flu. Anger is like a sickness that needs to be cured. They will apologize for their anger and begin damage control to salvage and repair any hurt feelings. They will go back to their office and start undoing. They will try to talk themselves out of their initial feelings and pretend that it really wasn't that important; it just isn't worth it. Women's greatest fear is that anger could cost them plenty, and they don't want to pay the high price of losing relationships. Nice girls don't do anger. Instead, women bury feelings, avoid, and accommodate. Women may sulk, give the silent treatment, complain to third parties about the other party, or make snide remarks—all indirect expressions of anger. These avoidance patterns significantly reduce any opportunity for the chance of productive conflict. When women go into this flight pattern and avoid, they jeopardize their relationships. A natural consequence is not as much interaction and the reduction of dependence.

Women suppress anger, and men express it.

Exercise 6.7. Women: The Queens of Passive-Aggressive Behavior

Women often express anger and frustration indirectly by using passive-aggressive behaviors. They appear innocent and socially acceptable on the surface, but underneath there is anger. The root cause of this behavior is believed to be the inability of women to express resentment and anger directly in a healthy manner, acceptable by everyone.

Goal

Identify how women present double messages and the impact of this on conflict management.

Objectives

- Understand how passive-aggressive behavior is communicated.

- Identify the role passive-aggressive behavior plays in how women handle conflict.

Timing of Exercise

15 minutes

Materials

Handout: Reflection for Women on Passive-Aggressive Behavior, chart paper and easel, markers

Slide 6.10

Setup

☐ Place participants in coed groups of five to eight.

☐ Distribute the handout.

☐ Ask the women participants in the groups to respond to the examples of passive-aggressive behavior.

☐ Ask the women if they can provide an example of this behavior at work.

Slide 6.10

WOMEN: The Queens of Passive-Aggressive Behavior

Source: Copyright © 2012 by Audrey Nelson and Claire Damken Brown.

Sample Handout Text: Reflection for Women on Passive-Aggressive Behavior

Do any of these items resonate with you?

- Forgetting appointments

- Saying unkind things and quickly apologizing

- Sarcasm

- Getting tearful when certain topics come up

- Convenient misunderstandings

- Slamming doors and professing nothing is wrong

- Acting helpless

- Causing situations so that others are inconvenienced

- Being tardy

- Disclosing private information and then apologizing

- Sarcastic sniping (hostile sarcasm)

- Convenient forgetfulness

- Silent treatment

- Crimes behind the scenes (sabotage work)

Debrief

The "cure" for eliminating passive-aggressive behavior is expressing anger directly. What can women do to mitigate a backlash in response to their anger? Often, providing a credible explanation for the anger is a simple, yet effective strategy. A simple explanation is a powerful thing. A statement that is straightforward, exempt from lengthy elaboration, works. Although situations at work occur in which anger is normal, women have to be careful because they walk a tightrope. Women walk a fine line between not being completely unemotional and appearing cold, and not displaying emotions such as anger that will harm them and have negative consequences. A woman can disagree without being disagreeable. She acknowledges the other person's idea and what they said, and then she presents her idea, backing it up with good reasons, logic, and data. If she gets the feeling that she is coming off too aggressively, she can add an invitation for the other person to participate: "What are your thoughts about my ideas?" Passive-aggressive behavior may appear innocent on the surface, but underneath the behavior, rage flows.

Women follow the rules, and men break the rules.

Exercise 6.8. Case Study: Women and the Challenge of Saying "No"

Goal

Identify how and why women need to learn to say "no."

Objectives

- Identify the underpinnings to women's inability to say "no."

- Analyze the importance for women of setting boundaries in conflict.

- Understand the connection between women's refraining from saying "no" and their need to be liked.

Timing of Exercise

15 minutes

Materials

Handout: Case Study: Genet Can't Say "No," chart paper and easel, markers

Setup

☐ Place the participants in coed groups of five to eight.

☐ The content for the handout includes the case study and questions. Distribute the handout and ask the groups to read and discuss the case study.

☐ Ask the women if they have a hard time saying "no" and in what situations.

☐ Ask the men if they have had any experiences with someone like Genet and what their reaction was.

☐ Ask the women if they can provide any examples of this behavior at work.

Case Study: Genet Can't Say "No"

Genet was the office manager of a small tech company of approximately three hundred employees. She received many daily requests regarding cubicle arrangements, supplies, ergonomic furniture, and computer and equipment needs. She had to deny some of the requests due to the budget and guidelines set forth by the company. Although she would carefully explain company policy guidelines to the employee making a request, she always felt guilty when she had to say "no." According to Genet, some of the requests were "over the top and some employees felt like they should have it all." But she still felt bad about saying "no" even to absurd requests. She claimed that "she had enough guilt to start her own religion." After refusing requests, she would check back with the employees to reassure herself that they still "liked" her.

Source: Copyright © 2012 by Audrey Nelson and Claire Damken Brown.

Debrief

So begins a self-perpetuating cycle that leads to other dysfunctional behaviors, such as guilt for saying "no." Women are so concerned about being nice (remember sugar and spice and everything nice) and the "Queen for a Day" that they want to be popular at any cost, even if it means forsaking their personal needs, such as setting boundaries and maintaining a sense of self. Women have a high need to please, to be liked and accepted. In conflict, it is an adaptation.

Rule Makers and Rule Breakers: Is There a Double Standard in Expressing Anger?

Girls and women are expected to comply with rules and socially controlled behavior far more rigidly than boys. When men break the rules in corporate America, they are mavericks, and when women break the rules, they cross the line. Male behavior enjoys a larger latitude of acceptance: boys will be boys.

Men have more latitude when it comes to expressing anger. It is a socially sanctioned emotion for them to express, and they often lose control faster than women. For a man to be explosive may fuel and assert his power and authority. People sit up and take notice. For men, anger can be the ultimate display of masculinity. Anger is bold and fearless. A man can demonstrate his dominance with aggressive displays.

Unfortunately, when they explode in anger, men can pay a high price by alienating others. Men's anger can take the form of criticizing others, using sarcasm to get a point across, storming out of the room, pounding a fist, and yelling. These tactics push people away, leave people angry, and put men in a more troubling situation. When men blow up at others at work, it may end up costing them more than they expected. However, there is considerable evidence that anger can often work in men's behalf to strengthen their image.

A study conducted by Deborah Cox (2000), a psychologist and assistant professor in the department of guidance and counseling at

Southwest Missouri State University and principal investigator, examined how men and women express their anger, as well as their tendency to act on their own behalf. Some psychologists believe that assertiveness and self-promoting behaviors, historically thought of as "masculine," are related to the ability to express anger outwardly and directly. The idea is that protecting one's rights and self-interests involves the ability to channel anger and create change; for example, by openly and publicly expressing displeasure verbally.

The researchers gave 80 men and 123 women a collection of five routine questionnaires used to assess anger expression and personality traits, such as assertiveness, self-esteem, sense of effectiveness, and expectations for success. Participants were volunteers from a variety of occupational and socioeconomic backgrounds recruited from schools, college campuses, retail businesses, churches, and other workplaces in the Midwest. The study subjects rated themselves on nearly two hundred traits and scenarios directly or indirectly related to anger expression and self-promotional "masculine" traits.

The researchers found that men felt less effective and less instrumental when forced to hold their anger in. In addition, they found a correlation between expressing one's anger outwardly and being assertive in men, but not in women. This finding is not surprising, since men are generally more assertive than women; expressing anger requires a self-confident, assertive style.

Men felt less effective when forced to hold their anger in.

According to Cox, men felt less effective overall when they reported an inward or suppressive style of expressing their anger, whereas for women, this relationship did not emerge.

As discussed earlier, women express anger indirectly through passive-aggressive behaviors, or they tend to repress it.

In another study, "Can an Angry Woman Get Ahead? Gender, Status Conferral, and Workplace Emotion Expression," published in *Psychological Science,* two social psychologists at the Yale School of Management, Victoria Brescoll and E. L. Uhlmann (2008), examined how people perceive men and women differently when they express anger at work (pp. 268–275). The participants, all working adults, watched a video of job interviews in which the men and women interviewees were asked to describe a time when something went wrong at work and whether it made them feel angry or sad. After watching the video, the participants were asked to rate the interviewees on factors such as their status and the salary they should earn. The angry man was perceived as higher status, more competent, and more likely to be hired and given the highest salary. The angry woman was viewed as lower status and less competent than both the angry and sad men, and also the sad woman. She was given a salary that was $14,000 less than the angry man's and $5,500 less than her sad female counterpart.

When women express anger, they experience
a backlash.

Brescoll and Okimoto's (2010) research examined anger as a status cue and found that people will give more status to men who express anger. They wanted to know if the same would hold true for women. They found that it does not; when women express anger at work they experience a backlash. The research suggests that female leaders suffer from expressing anger while male leaders benefit from the same behavior due to prescriptive gender stereotypes—beliefs about how men and women should behave. Women are expected to be kind, not angry, and they are punished if they violate this "prescription for behavior" (p. 924).

A final study conducted by Brescoll (2007) is worth mentioning. She wanted to conduct a study aimed at understanding whether some of these findings apply to real-world organizations. Will people conform to gender stereotypes of emotion-display rules? Will men express more anger than women? If anger confers more status for men, will men express more anger?

Anger confers more status for men.

To answer these questions, Brescoll looked at the U.S. Senate, a complex organization that is centered around status and power, and the senators' floor speeches are filmed. She taped twenty random days of C-SPAN's Senate coverage in 2005 and coded the intensity and frequency of anger in each floor speech. She also used a measure of power and status that ranked each senator based on factors such as position, influence, and legislative actions. Brescoll found gender differences in the Senate. Male senators displayed more anger in their floor speeches than female senators. "It was interesting how relatively unemotional some of the female senators were compared to the male senators. Regardless of how much power women have, they're still not expressing anger," Brescoll wrote (p. 932). The higher-status male senators also displayed more anger than their lower-status counterparts.

Section 5: Crying as a Female Trademark

Slide 6.11
Crying as a Female Trademark

Source: Copyright © 2012 by Audrey Nelson and Claire Damken Brown.

Women are taught to be "highly expressive"; that is, they can express all of their emotions, including crying. Emotions are a female trademark. All sorts of cultural influences determine who cries and with what frequency. In their book *It's Always Personal*, Kreamer and Thompson (2011) surveyed 1,200 working Americans. They found that age and gender play a role in freeness in crying: women younger than forty-five are ten times as likely to cry at work as men forty-five and older.

Men report having feelings just as often as women do. They just don't express them. Men are just as high as women in emotional awareness. However, men process and express emotions differently than women, and they have no road map for how to combine the masculine requirement of being strong with being emotional at the same time. A woman cries and a man loses his temper; that seems to be the pervasive theme in many conflicts. Men and women react differently; she shows her vulnerability and he must remain in control. Remember control is the partner to power; they are synonymous and inseparable. Men feel that "If I have control then I have power," and "When I am losing control, I am losing power."

> She shows her vulnerability, and he
> remains in control.

Exercise 6.9. Men, Women, and Emotional Display

Goal

Stimulate awareness of sex differences in emotional display and how it affects conflict management.

Objectives

- Increase awareness of gender differences in emotional display.

- Understand how sex differences in emotional display can affect conflict outcomes.

Timing of Exercise

10–15 minutes

Materials

Handout: The Emotional Continuum, chart paper and easel, markers

Setup

☐ Distribute the handout.

☐ Instruct the participants to plot themselves on the continuum by circling the number that best represents their emotional expression at work.

☐ Place the participants in coed groups of five to eight.

☐ Participants in the small groups answer and discuss the debrief questions that follow, and then you debrief the larger group by asking the same questions.

☐ Wrap up by soliciting key points from the small group.

Sample Handout Text: The Emotional Continuum

How do you measure up in expressing your emotions at work? Circle the number that reflects your emotional expression:

1. . . . . 2. . . . . 3. . . . . 4. . . . . 5. . . . . 6. . . . . 7. . . . . 8. . . . . 9. 10

Low   Moderate   High

Debrief

• Did you circle a number in the "low," "moderate," or "high" section?

• How would that number vary if you were at home with family, versus at work with coworkers, or with a group of total strangers? Why?

- How would that number vary if you were in a group of all men, all women, or men and women? Why?

- Would the number you selected be different if your direct supervisor were present? Why? Would it matter if your direct supervisor were the same sex as you or the opposite sex? Why or why not?

- Compare the discussions and comments from men and women. Do most women indicate responding in one direction while most men indicate they are responding in another direction? Why or why not?

For women, expressing emotions, especially crying, is tricky business. She risks being perceived by others, especially men, as weak, emotional, and unreliable. Men and women may also perceive her as manipulative. She is using tears to get her way or make us feel sorry for her.

Women's tears are seldom an expression of sadness, but rather of anger.

In *Code Switching: How to Talk So Men Will Listen* (C. Brown and Nelson, 2009), the authors present a useful technique for women in this kind of situation: precuing. "Set up the conflict communication, and possible tears, for a win. Tell the person that you're very concerned and upset about what you're preparing to discuss. If you subsequently get upset, say that you will take responsibility for your tears and you want him to take responsibility for what you are saying. Many women have reported that when they indicate that they may 'lose it' and start to cry, they actually gain a sense of more control and end up not crying" (p. 137).

This precuing technique handles the credibility issue for women and also eliminates the perception of manipulation. Men know that the tears are a product of concern and frustration.

One of the biggest mistakes men make in conflict is that they perceive a woman's tears as an indication of sadness. He may begin to console her only to be told to back off, because he has misread the cue. Underneath a woman's tears is seldom sadness, but rather anger. At this point, many men feel a high level of discomfort with her tears.

Exercise 6.10. Men and Emotions

Goal

Identify why men ignore the emotional dimension of the conflict and the potential impact that this can have on resolution.

Objectives

- Analyze how and why men stay focused on the content or issues in a conflict and ignore the emotions and feelings.

- Identify the impact the male style could have in contrast to women's focus on the emotional dimension of a conflict.

- Define how the refusal to engage is a way to maintain power and control in a conflict.

Timing of Exercise

15 minutes

Materials

Handout: Men and Emotions: Reflection for Men, chart paper and easel, markers

Slide 6.12

Setup

☐ Place participants in coed groups of five to eight.

☐ Distribute the handout.

☐ Ask the male participants in the groups to respond to the examples.

☐ Ask the men if they can provide an example of this behavior at work.

Slide 6.12

MEN: The Hermit Crab or Refusal to Engage

Source: Copyright © 2012 by Audrey Nelson and Claire Damken Brown.

Sample Handout Text: Reflection for Men: Men and Emotions

Do any of these claims resonate with you?

• Retreat and clam up when things become emotional

• Resent when someone asks you how you are feeling

• Avoid conflict encounters that you believe may involve sharing feelings

• Try to stick with facts and don't address feelings

• Try not to pay too much attention to other people's feelings during a conflict

• Feel it is safer to keep things "logical"

Debrief

Men can become like hermit crabs, refusing to engage. They pull in when they feel threatened or when they begin to lose control in a conflict. Men often score high in both competition and avoidance on the Thomas-Kilmann Conflict Mode Instrument (TKI). This seemingly contradictory result makes sense. The man will compete when he thinks he can win, but avoid it when he senses that he can lose.

Men don't want to be bullied or cajoled into sharing emotions.

Men don't want to be bullied or cajoled into sharing emotions. They feel more comfortable with report talk, not rapport talk. A man prefers to "report" the circumstances and offer logical and unemotional ideas. A woman wants to talk about her feelings and, most important, check on the status of the relationship through rapport talk. When a woman is engaged in conflict, she needs reassurance that the relationship is still intact. Women often perform a lot of relationship maintenance during a conflict.

Slide 6.13

Men Play the Devil's Advocate

Source: Copyright © 2012 by Audrey Nelson and Claire Damken Brown.

Men want solutions to problems, and women look for understanding of their problems. Men believe expressing disagreement is a sign of intimacy. Women think expressing disagreement is a threat to intimacy. Men like to play the devil's advocate, and women want to help everyone agree in discussion. There's no right or wrong to these approaches, just differences.

Men often enjoy fighting. Fighting has a different emotional meaning for men than for women. For men, fighting can be a positive experience that can bring them together with others. Men often complain that women don't understand *when it is over, it is over.* A man in a seminar once said, "I cannot stand fighting with a woman. Women never get it that once the fight is over, we are done." Men can duke it out in the Monday morning staff meeting, and then you can see them in the company lunch room later that day having lunch together laughing and having a good time. Men use anger to influence each other.

The goal of fighting for men is to display their skill at winning within the rules. Our culture has a long and rich tradition of fighting fair. Women can observe the winners and losers when men fight. How long did they stay angry? Usually, not long. Testing, sparring, and sometimes yelling and being aggressive can be a part of the game. For most women, aggressiveness has a negative connotation. Although aggression can mean hostility and intimidation, it can also mean determined, firm, bold, and resolute. The latter is admired and often builds credibility.

Slide 6.14

Women Internalize Criticism and Men Externalize Criticism

Source: Copyright © 2012 by Audrey Nelson and Claire Damken Brown.

Women tend to take things personally in conflict. Women can be more sensitive to criticism. No one likes being criticized. But when someone criticizes a man, he reacts in one of a couple of ways. Men will argue against the criticism or just take it and be done with it. Men externalize criticism and women internalize it. Women get stuck on the critique, remember it, and ruminate about it. In *How Men Think: The Seven Essential Rules for Making It in a Man's World* (Mendell, 1996), the author summarizes childhood sex differences in the socialization of making mistakes and taking criticism:

> Little boys play a lot of competitive sports.
>
> Little girls play dolls.
>
> Little boys make a lot of mistakes playing team sports.
>
> Little girls can't make a lot of mistakes playing dolls because there are no rules.
>
> When a boy makes a mistake, he is encouraged to go back and try harder.
>
> When girls make mistakes, they are comforted.
>
> Boys learn that making a mistake may be embarrassing but not fatal.
>
> Girls learn mistakes are something to feel bad about.
>
> Boys learn that you earn your team's respect by striving to improve your skills after making a mistake.
>
> Girls learn you will be consoled if you call attention to your mistakes [p. 127].

Finally, women sympathize with each other when they make mistakes and may be overly apologetic. "I am sorry" is heard more in women's vocabulary than men's vocabulary. In contrast, men think mistakes should receive a brief acknowledgment, be rectified, and then be forgotten. No one in business gets a bonus for calling attention to a mistake. By calling attention to their mistakes, women build a reputation for incompetence. Listen to men around the water cooler. Men don't hesitate to share their successes and victories while minimizing their mistakes. In addition, men will be accused of not taking ownership or responsibility for the error, and women can be perceived as taking ownership by making it personal.

Science has also uncovered sex differences in brain functioning. The female brain isn't designed to compartmentalize personal feelings in the same way a man's brain does. He can put it on the shelf and separate it; this helps him distance himself from what might otherwise be an uncomfortable situation. He can turn off the switch of emotions. This serves him, because it's difficult for him to think clearly when faced with emotions.

One of men's subconscious unwritten rules is that people should leave their feelings on the sidewalk and not carry them into work. When a man observes a woman taking something personally, he views her as less business savvy and as someone who operates more on emotions than on logic.

Slide 6.15

Managing Conflict Successfully

Moving beyond the rejection of sex differences and accepting that each style of handling conflict has some merit and can be managed is critical to managing conflict for a positive outcome for both women and men.

Source: Copyright © 2012 by Audrey Nelson and Claire Damken Brown.

The workplace will always have conflict, which can assume many forms, from small encounters to full-scale battles between men and women. Where there are people and relationships, conflict is inevitable. One of the hallmark signs of a successful organization is the ability to work through the conflict. One of the keys to managing conflict successfully requires an understanding of how women and men handle conflict and how to channel these differences for a productive outcome. When men and women come together at work, they each bring their distinctive style of handling conflict, and often their styles clash and result in a lot of confusion. Moving beyond the rejection of sex differences and accepting that each style of handling conflict has some merit and can be managed is critical to creating more victors than victims and managing the conflict for a constructive result for both women and men.

Refer to this book's Additional Instruments and Training Tools section, for Chapter Six, for other exercises and discussion tools on conflict and gender.

Use the Action Steps slides for men and women as part of your summary for the material you presented from this chapter.

Slide 6.16

Action Steps for Men

- Minimize or refrain from bantering with women.

- Acknowledge that other styles besides competition have value and a use in conflict.

- Incorporate and acknowledge the emotional dimension in conflict.

- Encourage women to disagree and reaffirm the relationship at the same time.

- Offer understanding and empathy.

- Refrain from refusing to engage in conflict when you feel you cannot win.

Source: Copyright © 2012 by Audrey Nelson and Claire Damken Brown.

Slide 6.17

Action Steps for Women

- Realize that men play fight, and they are not attacking you.

- Incorporate more *report talk* and focus on the issues in a conflict.

- Express disagreement, say "no," and challenge ideas.

- Directly express disappointment and anger.

- Offer solutions to problems.

- Use the precuing technique when you think you may start crying.

Source: Copyright © 2012 by Audrey Nelson and Claire Damken Brown.

CHAPTER 7

He and She Wired

I am announcing a ban on e-mail every Friday to and from all sales and operation associates, effective immediately.

—Jay M. Ellison, Executive Vice President and Chief Operating Officer, U.S. Cellular Corporation (2004)

Learning Objectives

- Examine gender differences in e-mail.

- Identify women's use of emoticons, lexical surrogates, and exclamation points.

- Compare the similarity in speech and linguistic gender differences to e-mail preferences.

- Understand how e-mail style can affect credibility, especially for women.

- Understand how men's e-mail style can be interpreted by women as abrupt and inconsiderate.

- Discuss how women can use e-mail to minimize interruptions and overlapping.

- Identify how women can utilize e-mail as a conflict-management tool.

Introduction

To make the best use of all associates' time and to encourage employees to engage with one another on a more frequent basis, then-Executive Vice President and COO of U.S. Cellular Corporation Jay Ellison announced a ban on e-mail every Friday for all sales and operations associates. That memo went into effect in August 2004. U.S. Cellular Corporation is based in Chicago; at the time of this memo, the company had more than five hundred retail locations nationwide and seven thousand employees. Ellison's goal was to increase face time among employees. Making time for face time is certainly a mantra for the twenty-first century (Horng, 2007).

Regardless of the value of meeting people face-to-face, our reliance on e-mail, the Internet, texting, and other forms of computer-generated communication is not going away. It is here to stay and is an integral part of the fabric of societies and businesses worldwide.

Although e-mail is used extensively, it still lacks universally agreed-on modes of behavior established by generations of use and the precise means for conveying the exact impressions the e-mail sender wishes to convey. And this is very evident in the gender differences exhibited in the composition, length, and use of emoticons, greetings, exclamation points, and lexical surrogates. Because e-mail is a major form of communication in the business world and there is a lot of confusion in the style and interpretation of e-mail between women and men, an examination of gender styles is warranted.

Timing for Unit

30–45 minutes

Materials for Unit

Handouts, chart paper and easel, markers

Slides 7.1 through 7.9.

Section 1: He and She: The Smiley Face Dilemma

Exercise 7.1. Is There a Gender Difference in the Use of Emoticons?

Goal

To examine the impact of the gender-based use of emoticons in e-mail.

Objectives

- Increase the awareness of the use of emoticons in e-mail communication.

- Understand the relationship of emoticons and emotional expressiveness.

- Identify how women's use of emoticons affects credibility.

- Identify how men's lack of emoticons affects relationships with women.

Timing of Exercise

10–15 minutes

Materials

Handout: Gender and Emoticons, chart paper and easel, markers

Slide 7.1

Setup

☐ Break into coed groups.

☐ The content for the handout is the same as the content on the slide. Distribute the handout.

☐ Instruct the participants to circle emoticons they use in e-mail correspondence at work.

☐ Have the groups compare what emoticons they circled and identify gender correlations.

☐ Bring the discussion to the large group and have the small groups share their observations.

Slide 7.1

Gender and Emoticons

Circle the emoticons you use in e-mails:

Emoticon	Meaning
:-)	Smile
;-)	Wink
:-(	Frown
:-o	Shocked
:-\	Puzzled
:-/	Skeptical
:-l	Indifferent
:'-(	Crying
:-@	Screaming
:-&	Tongue-tied
:-D	Laughing
:-c	Dismayed

Source: Copyright © 2012 by Audrey Nelson and Claire Damken Brown.

Debrief

The facilitator provides questions for group processing and discussion points. Every individual group gets an opportunity to share their findings.

The facilitator asks the large group the following questions with discussion points that can be added to the group's observations (the group offers their observations first and then the facilitator adds discussion points):

1. What was the most-used emoticon for women? Take a show of hands from women who use emoticons in work e-mails.

   - Most likely women will say they use the smiley face the most, and the majority of women will raise their hand, reflecting a higher use than men of emoticons.

   - Several studies found that women used emoticons more often than men did (Witmer & Katzman, 1997; Wolf, 2000; and Baron, 2004).

   - Research also reveals that women use more smiley and laughing emoticons (Baron, 2004).

2. What was the most-used emoticon for men? Take a show of hands from men who use emoticons.

   - Very few men, if any, use emoticons. Expect one or two and, most likely, no men to raise their hands.

   - We are hard pressed to think of an e-mail we've received from a male colleague or coworker that used emoticons.

3. How do women in the group use emoticons? What purpose does it serve in the e-mail message?

   - Women incorporate emoticons for several purposes: to soften or mitigate a message, for relationship building, and to express how they feel.

4. What purpose does an emoticon serve for men?

- Point out the irony that emoticons were originally created by Scott Fahlman, and his intent was to banter, tease, and make jokes—not the same purposes for which women use emoticons.

- Basically, the emoticon serves little purpose for men. The goal of their e-mails is task-oriented, getting down to business. Men often report that emoticons are a waste of time and rarely notice them in an e-mail message. They are looking for that answer, not to connect or build a relationship. Furthermore, from a man's perspective, emoticons jeopardize the sender's credibility. In short, incorporating an emoticon is a negative. However, would incorporating emoticons in e-mails to women have any positive impact on building relationships with them? Possibly.

The term *emoticons*—short for "emotion icons"—refers to graphic signs, such as smiley faces :) and laughs out loud (LOL), which often accompany computer communication. They are most often characterized as iconic indicators of emotion, conveyed through a communication channel that is parallel to the linguistic one. Emoticons are used in e-mails, blogs, instant messaging (IM), and bulletin-board postings.

The introduction of graphic signs to printed text made its debut in 1982 via a computer scientist at Carnegie Mellon University, Scott Fahlman. His original intention was to signal that something was a joke (or not) in messages posted to a computer science discussion forum (Krohn, 2004). This intent parallels men's predisposition to engage in linguistic banter.

The majority of emoticons mimic facial expressions. Signs such as the sideways smiley face originated in Western culture and are used in Western-culture contexts, while other signs are specific to other cultural contexts, such as Japanese *kaomoji* (literally, "facemarks"), which are viewed straight on, ^_^ (Katsuno & Yano, 2007).

Emoticons are conceived of as nonverbal indicators of emotion. They attempt to substitute what is missing from computer-generated communication: the emotional dimension that is primarily communicated through facial expressions. They have the power to soften, add to, or intensify the meaning of the message.

How and Why He and She Use Emoticons

Slide 7.2

How and Why He and She Use Emoticons

And whatever you do, don't use emoticons when sending e-mail to a man.

Source: Copyright © 2012 by Audrey Nelson and Claire Damken Brown.

Can you remember the last time you received an e-mail from a male colleague, coworker, or client that had a smiley face emoticon? In contrast, women in Internet Relay Chat channels incorporated three times as many representations of smiling and laughing emoticons than men (Herring, 2003). This is illustrative of women's need to soften the message and build relationship.

Men seldom incorporate emoticons in their e-mails.

In contrast, however, men used emoticons more often to express sarcasm or to banter. Wolf (2000) makes a point that males use smileys for the purposes of expressing sarcasm and teasing more often than females do. In other words, when a man does employ emoticons it is a specific kind of emotional display. Wolf suggested:

> What emerges on a closer inspection, however, is that while emoticons are defined as vehicles to express emotion—hence "emotional icons"—their actual function hinges on the definition of the word emotion. While it can be argued that sarcasm and teasing, for example, derive from or comprise different emotions, whether they constitute an emotion is debatable [p. 832].

Men use emoticons in their e-mails to banter
and express sarcasm.

Slide 7.3

How and Why He and She Use Emoticons

Women will often use emoticons to soften the blow of negative feedback or mitigate a conflict.

Source: Copyright © 2012 by Audrey Nelson and Claire Damken Brown.

Women will often use emoticons to soften the blow of negative feedback or mitigate a conflict. A woman may relay a criticism or point of contention, but can soften the message by adding a smiley face: "Remember those stats were due yesterday. :)" In addition, for women the absence of an emoticon can indicate a lack of emotion and, in that, a lack of information, especially if the sender is another woman. The exclusion of the ubiquitous (autotext) smiley face at the end of her message would be like wiping away the ever-present female smile or punctuation of laughter at the end of a sentence. A word of warning for women: pay attention to when and to whom you send emoticons, especially at work. A smiley face emoticon in an e-mail to the boss may be interpreted as not taking your job seriously, affecting your credibility.

Women use emoticons in their e-mails to build relationships and soften the message.

For the most part, computers are a nonverbally impoverished "lean" medium, which makes it challenging to create a sense of social presence and convey the interpersonal cues so important to creating and maintaining an emotional connection and building relationships with colleagues. Women's nonverbal repertoire mimics their e-mail style in an attempt to meet these interpersonal needs.

One example is women sending double messages and builds on discussions that examine how women say one thing but do something else nonverbally. This chapter may be combined with Chapter Four, "Women, Men, and Unspoken Messages," which examines the relationship between the nonverbal and verbal component and women punctuating a serious message with a giggle or a smile. In short, what is communicated in verbal and nonverbal communication channels is replicated in e-mail communication. The same gender patterns emerge through a different medium.

Finally, while there are similarities and obvious comparisons that facial expressions mimic the repertoire of emoticon facial expressions, it should be emphasized that facial expressions are often unintentional and emoticons are intentional. In other words, emoticons are produced consciously and intentionally similar to written language. Facial expressions are given off more on a low level of awareness and, often, spontaneously.

Another effect displayed online by women is the use of lexical surrogates. Lexical surrogates are typed representations of vocalized sounds such as "hmmmm," "soooooo," or "grrrrrr." Elongated words are also lexical surrogates (for example, "I love this new assignment sooooooooooo much"), often emphasizing certain words as a display of emotion. Such devices are thought to substitute symbols for the missing nonverbal behaviors to add socioemotional content to women's messages.

Finally, it has been reported that exclamation points are typically used by females significantly more than by males (Colley & Todd, 2002). When considered in relation to gender, exclamation points are often described as "markers of excitability," a phrase that implies instability and emotional randomness. It is an intensifier signalling "I really mean this!" Men affirm their views or opinions by simply asserting them. No explanation point is necessary. Men sometimes interpret both lexical surrogates and exclamation points as nonessentials. The incorporation of these relational and expressive elements can serve to weaken the impact and credibility of the woman's message.

Women employ more lexical surrogates
and exclamation points.

Exercise 7.2. Is There a Credibility Gap in Her E-Mail Style?

Goal

Examine the impact of lexical surrogates and exclamation points on credibility in an e-mail.

Objectives

- Increase the awareness of the impact of lexical surrogates and exclamation points in e-mail communication.

- Identify how women's use of lexical surrogates and exclamation points affects credibility.

Timing of Exercise

5–10 minutes

Materials

Chart paper and easel, markers

Slide 7.4

Setup

☐ Conduct this as a large-group exercise.

☐ Ask the group to view the slide.

☐ Ask them which e-mail is more professional? Why?

Slide 7.4
Her and His E-Mails

Her e-mail:

> Working with this team is soooooo chaotic!!! They are not aligned on the budget and it is nerve-wracking. Grrrrrr!

His e-mail:

> This team is unorganized and not aligned on the budget.

Source: Copyright © 2012 by Audrey Nelson and Claire Damken Brown.

Debrief

There are several perspectives one can take on the e-mail gender-style differences. A woman might feel that her e-mail is entertaining and personable. She is being open and honest about how she feels. However, the men in the audience may have the reaction: "Don't waste my time" or "This e-mail isn't businesslike."

Ask the group: "What is the solution?" Should the woman accommodate the man and omit the exclamation points and lexical surrogates? Or should he just go along with her style? Is this also a professional issue? Does the woman's style affect her credibility? Could it be perceived that she can't handle the team?

Section 2: E-Mail Showdown: One Sentence Versus One Paragraph

All of us experience a distinct style difference in our e-mail correspondence with men and women. Men's e-mails, like their conversations, tend to be short, abbreviated, and to the point. A few of our favorite e-mails sent by men are one to three words: *let's do it, go for it, yup, Roger that, okay, done, no, yes, all systems go,* and *ditto.* One could argue that men are even more to-the-point in e-mail than in speech. Men are goal- and task-oriented. In the man's mind, shorter is better and e-mail is a tool for efficiency and nothing else.

Another aspect of e-mail reveals women as more process-oriented. While both sexes are focused on the same end result, each will express status differently: the woman describing the process and the man describing in a direct manner the end result or goal. The woman will often include details that the man considers unimportant and unnecessary.

training tip

Again, Chapter Two, "He Speaks, She Speaks: What Different Things They Say," can be used to draw out similarities in the gender styles of speech and e-mail. For example, women's speech is process-oriented and therefore usually longer than men's speech. Both men's speech and e-mail tend to be short and often in bullet style. In addition, women employ more bonding and relationship-building patterns in their speech, and the same is evident in their e-mail, such as incorporating emoticons, exclamation points, and lexical surrogates.

Exercise 7.3. Case Study: Her Process Format Versus His Goal Format

Goal

Identify how women use a process e-mail style and men use a goal-oriented e-mail style.

Objectives

- Understand how e-mail styles can be interpreted differently.

- Analyze alternative e-mail styles in terms of efficiency and credibility.

Timing of Exercise

10–15 minutes

Materials

Handout: Case Study: Her Process Format Versus His Goal Format, chart paper and easel, markers

Setup

☐ Place participants in coed groups of five to eight.

☐ The content for the handout includes the case study and questions. Distribute the handout.

☐ Ask the participants to read the case study and answer the questions.

☐ Ask each group to assign a scribe who will take notes on the group's answers to the questions.

☐ Address each question with the entire class and solicit the individual group answers.

Case Study: Her Process Format Versus His Goal Format

Her Format: The Process

I spoke with the SIU investigator to let him know that Mr. Insured has "lawyered up," and the EUOs have been postponed. He told me that he received a certified letter "purported" to be from Mr. Insured, asking for copies of reports. He forwarded the letter to Ms. Client to forward to us for handling.

After I spoke with Mr. Investigator, I was wandering through Parties and realized that Mr. Independent Adjuster was the person I was supposed to contact, not Mr. Investigator. I advised Mr. Independent Adjuster of the "lawyering up" and Mr. Insured's request for postponement of 30 days. Mr. Independent Adjuster may be in the hospital in 30 days. He has a suspected aorta aneurysm and will be having open heart surgery. He will keep us advised.

Court reporter has been advised of postponement.

His Format: The Goal

Mission accomplished.

Source: Brown & Nelson, 2009, p. 86.

Questions

1. Did you prefer reading the man's or the woman's e-mail? Why?

2. Are the details in the woman's e-mail important considerations?

3. Is the woman's credibility jeopardized by a lengthier description of the outcome?

4. Did you feel you had enough information with the man's e-mail?

5. Would you feel compelled to answer her e-mail or his e-mail? Why?

Debrief

Since women tend to use a facilitative communication style, seeking dialogue, they communicate by including details that can make an e-mail rich in facts and sometimes provide necessary background information. In contrast, men, being more prone to a restricting style of communication, seem to feel one word or sentence is sufficient. If it answers the question and concern in one sentence, it works.

A study, "Yakity-Yak: Who Talks Back? An E-Mail Experiment," conducted at California State University, Fullerton, asked the question, "Who talks more—men or women?" by analyzing gender differences in talking via electronic communication (Brajer & Gill, 2010). The researchers found that women used on average 26.9 percent more words than men.

Section 3: Why Can't He Be Nice?

Often men's e-mails do not begin with "dear" or sign off with "sincerely" or "best regards," which are more pervasive in women's e-mails. Women's e-mails often contain an acknowledgment of appreciation, a "thank-you" or "please." Women also incorporate good wishes, "have a nice day," "enjoy your weekend," or "hope your week is going well."

Women have more positive attitudes toward using e-mail as a tool to connect with others. They find sending e-mail more enjoyable and useful for maintaining good relations than men do. Men tend to favor assertive as opposed to affiliative speech and e-mail makes a perfect vehicle for this goal. For men, e-mail is simply a tool to dispense information and nothing more.

Thanking, whether of the friendly or effusive type, also tends to be a predominantly female behavior. These findings are consistent with Herring's (1994) observation that female online discourse style is characterized by "supportiveness," which includes "expressions of appreciation, thanking, and community building activities that make other participants feel accepted and welcome" (p. 4). Again, this kind of maintenance and acknowledgment is usually not considered by men in the composition of their e-mails.

Men seldom employ greetings or closing salutations in their e-mails.

Exercise 7.4. Case Study: Why Can't He Be Nice?

Goal

Identify how men use an abbreviated e-mail style that often excludes a greeting or closing salutation.

Objectives

- Understand how men's e-mail style can be interpreted by women.

- Analyze men's e-mail style in terms of efficiency and relationship maintenance.

Timing of Exercise

10–15 minutes

Materials

Handout: Case Study: Can He Be Both "Nice" and Efficient?, chart paper and easel, markers

Slide 7.5

Setup

☐ Place the participants in coed groups of five to eight.

☐ The content for the handout includes the case study and questions. Distribute the handout.

☐ Ask the participants to read the case study and answer the questions.

☐ Ask each group to assign a scribe who will take notes on the group's answers to the questions.

☐ Address each question with the entire class and solicit the individual group answers.

Slide 7.5

Why Can't He Be Nice?

Often men's e-mails do not begin with "dear" or sign off with "sincerely" or "best regards," which are more pervasive in women's e-mails.

Source: Copyright © 2012 by Audrey Nelson and Claire Damken Brown.

Case Study: Can He Be Both "Nice" and Efficient?

Audrey knew a male manager who disclosed the impact an e-mail he sent had on a long-time female employee. He said he was going fast and forgot to start with "Dear" and simply wrote two sentences about the due date and logistics of a project. Later in the day, he encountered this woman and she asked him if he was mad at her. He was perplexed because his intent was to be goal oriented and get the business done, not to "sugarcoat" his request. For her, she wanted only one word: "Dear." Or a "thanks." That would have taken care of the "relational" dimension of the e-mail that she needed.

Source: C. Brown & Nelson, 2009, p. 85.

Questions

1. Do you prefer an e-mail with a salutation? Do you think it is important?

2. Are a man's relationships jeopardized by omitting a greeting or a salutation?

3. Can a man's intent be potentially misread by omitting a greeting or a salutation?

Debrief

Solicit the small groups' answers to the questions and process them in the large group. E-mail correspondence that is neutral, that is, just states the facts or outlines the task, tends to be interpreted negatively, especially by women. Thus there is no such thing as a neutral e-mail message. Although the intent may be simply to transmit a task message with no affect or emotional component, this kind of message will be interpreted as disapproving. Hence we have a dilemma with men's task-oriented style that excludes any positive comment, greeting, or gratitude. The man's intention is not to insult or be rude, just to be efficient. However, women, who are more relationship-oriented, are generally more comfortable with some greeting or positive accolade. One could argue it only takes a few seconds to include a "thanks" or "dear."

Section 4: Can E-Mail Level the Playing Field for Women?

Slide 7.6

Can E-Mail Level the Playing Field for Women?

Source: Copyright © 2012 by Audrey Nelson and Claire Damken Brown.

Electronic communications may level the playing field, or even give females an advantage, in certain communication situations. Because of the one-way communication nature of e-mail, it eliminates the interruptions and monopolizing of airtime that so often prevail in the Monday morning staff meeting. The woman often struggles to get her point across only to be interrupted or have someone talk over her. It requires assertive skills to maintain and keep the floor, balanced with the social pressure to maintain face—both for the interrupter and the interrupted—and preserve everyone's dignity.

This can be a tough and exhausting exercise for many women. E-mail offers a woman the opportunity for expression without interruption. She can make her point without someone, usually a man, interrupting her.

In addition, a woman can convey thoughts and feelings in an e-mail that she may find nearly impossible to say aloud. She can keep control of the conversational flow and be more assertive than she could be in face-to-face encounters. E-mail is less inhibiting for many women. If a woman can't make her point in that meeting, she has the option for follow-up with an e-mail to conduct damage control or, often, to get attention and credibility for her ideas. This may result in a beneficial distance for women who want to minimize conflict and take the emotional charge off loaded emotional situations. E-mail can provide a woman with a voice when she feels voiceless in the Monday morning staff meeting.

training tip

Chapter Three, "Gender Conversation Technicalities," can be combined with this chapter. The degree of interruption behavior, overlapping, and yielding the floor to women become nonissues with e-mail as a channel of communication. Who gets airtime and acknowledgment for their ideas gets credibility; it is critical for women's success.

In addition, Chapter Six, "Men, Women, and Conflict," can be included for discussion concerning the benefits and ease of addressing conflict issues in an e-mail rather than face-to-face for women. It is much easier for a woman to confront conflict issues in an e-mail. It removes the emotional charge that accompanies face-to-face interactions. E-mail is a viable option that curtails women's predisposition to avoid or accommodate in conflict situations.

Slide 7.7

He and She Wired

- Women tend to use e-mail as an extension of the way they talk—process-oriented and to build rapport.

- Men tend to use e-mail in a briefer and more utilitarian style, with emphasis on reporting and task orientation.

Source: Copyright © 2012 by Audrey Nelson and Claire Damken Brown.

In general, women and men tend to use the e-mail medium as an extension of the way they talk. Women are more process-oriented with longer dialogue and more emotional and relational messages, to connect with people and build rapport. A woman will incorporate more emotional expressiveness in e-mail by using emoticons, lexical surrogates, and exclamation points. Such devices are thought to substitute symbols for the missing nonverbal behaviors in order to add socioemotional content to their messages. Men often perceive these elements as nonessential and trivializing, therefore weakening, the credibility of her message.

In speech and e-mail, men incline toward a briefer, more utilitarian style, which is focused on the instrumental and functional aspects of the message. Men emphasize more reporting than building rapport with others. Consequently, women may perceive men's e-mails as rude, abrupt, and unappreciative.

Use the Action Steps slides (on pages 239 and 240) for men and women as part of your summary for the material you presented from this chapter.

Slide 7.8
Action Steps for Men

- Refrain from using emoticons as banter in e-mails to women.

- Use emoticons to build relationships with women.

- Include a minimum of one of the following: a greeting, salutation or acknowledgment, and gratitude in e-mails to women.

- Include more detail and information in e-mails to women.

Source: Copyright © 2012 by Audrey Nelson and Claire Damken Brown.

Slide 7.9

Action Steps for Women

- Refrain from using emoticons in e-mails to men.

- Be aware that if a man incorporates emoticons, it is usually for banter.

- Regard exclamation points and lexical surrogates as nonessentials for men and omit them.

- Make e-mails to men as short as possible.

- Use e-mail as a medium for expressing conflict issues.

- Use e-mail to convey ideas and opinions if a woman feels she is not being heard in face-to-face encounters.

Source: Copyright © 2012 by Audrey Nelson and Claire Damken Brown.

CHAPTER 8

Final Thoughts on Reaching Across the Gender Divide

There should be no sense on reading this that one style is better, more logical, or more socially useful than another; both, and mixtures of both, are needed in different circumstances. Women must be more flexible—and so must men.

—Robin Lakoff (1975, p. 83)

Learning Objectives

- Provide different options for closing the training program.

- Review what participants learned about women's and men's communication styles.

- Move forward using a code-switching and androgynous communication style.

Introduction

The closing of the seminar presents an opportunity for the facilitator to review the program's key learning points, emphasize the choices participants have to create change, and identify next steps to enhance their communication style. Throughout the program, the facilitator talked with the participants about the advantages of having an increased number of communication tools in their tool kits. These tools represent the opportunities men and women have to learn from each other's communication style, make adjustments, and code switch, selecting the feminine or masculine communication behavior that best suits the situation and their needs. The closing reminds participants that they can create change; they have the knowledge and skills to improve their workplace communication with members of the opposite sex. The facilitator suggests that participants use their new communication tools and androgynous communication style to their career advantage.

Timing for Unit

10 to 30 minutes

Materials for Unit

Handouts, chart paper and easel, markers

Slides 8.1 through 8.6

Options for Closing the Training Program

The facilitator has a few options for how she or he chooses to close the program. Options include:

- Verbally providing a short summary

- Discussing a slide with the program's key learning points

- Discussing the handout with the program's key learning points

- Leading a short exercise that helps participants think about their key learning points

- Using any combination of the above

The option(s) chosen depend on the length of the program. For example, for a one-hour seminar, the facilitator may take a few minutes at the program's end to verbally summarize two or three key learning points. For a full-day program, the facilitator may choose to take the last thirty minutes to review and discuss the key learning points with participants by using an exercise, slide, and handout.

This "Final Thoughts" chapter concludes the training program. Unlike previous chapters, this is not a stand-alone chapter. As facilitator, use your discretion to select slides or exercises from this chapter that you think work best to close your program.

Closing the Program

The following slides (slides 8.1 through 8.3) can be used alone, together, or with other exercises in this chapter. The facilitator may display the slide and then summarize the items on the slide, or summarize the items first and then display the slide.

Men and women will continue to work together in the workplace. Women comprise more than 50 percent of the workforce and are

Slide 8.1
Take Charge!

Improve how women and men communicate:

- Understand the differences.

- Value the differences.

- Borrow from each other.

- Avoid the blame game.

- Be a diplomat.

Source: Copyright © 2012 by Audrey Nelson and Claire Damken Brown.

growing in their presence in management and executive levels. More so than women, men tend to be seen as the workplace power brokers. Understanding different communication styles is the first step men and women can take to promote a supportive workplace for both sexes. Valuing or appreciating the differences is important. Men are not being asked to stop being men; likewise, women are not being asked to stop being women. The androgynous communication style grasps the differences and uses them to improve the interactions between men and women. Borrowing from each style is like having the best of both worlds at your fingertips; the masculine and feminine communication behaviors are readily available to improve your communication with the opposite sex.

Women and men must move beyond blaming each other for poor communication, thoughtlessness in terms of speaking style, or labeling men's or women's behaviors as bad or "less than." Men and women must take the high road and be diplomatic, helping each other move beyond gender and workplace stereotypes. By using a code-switching and androgynous communication style, men and women can communicate better while creating a more equitable workplace. Breaking away from communication stereotypes allows both women and men to be more productive for their companies and ultimately reach their career goals.

> By using a code-switching and androgynous communication style, men and women can communicate better while creating a more equitable workplace.

Slide 8.2

Women and Men

Become self-conscious—self-monitor.

Stop the blame game.

Question the status quo.

Broaden your communication tool kit: use an androgynous style.

Source: Copyright © 2012 by Audrey Nelson and Claire Damken Brown.

For discussion, the facilitator can draw from the information about the first slide. Women and men benefit by monitoring their own behavior: watching or being conscious of their own verbal and nonverbal communication behaviors. For example, look for smiling inappropriately in situations or other double messages and adjust the

communication behavior to be congruent. Question how men
and women operate in the workplace. Question what has existed as
women's or men's communication styles and look for ways to code
switch, adopting the other's style to improve your communication.
Focus on developing the participants' communication tool kits. By
understanding and becoming comfortable with adapting an
androgynous style, an individual increases his or her interaction skills.
The more skills an individual has, the better able he or she is to adapt
and lead in various situations.

Change for the Better

In closing, facilitators may discuss items from slide 8.3 with the
participants as a reminder of the day's key points. The ultimate goal is
to change the workplace for the better in terms of how men and
women communicate with each other. The facilitator may choose to
add another key point to the slide's bulleted list or substitute for an
existing item with a key point of his or her choosing.

Use an androgynous communication style to
maximize your leadership skills and flexibility.

Slide 8.3
Change for the Better

- Code switch and use an androgynous communication style to maximize your communication with the opposite sex.

- Use an androgynous communication style to maximize your leadership skills and flexibility.

- Women: Integrate an androgynous communication style to improve your credibility and how you and your messages are received and perceived.

- Men: Integrate an androgynous communication style to improve your relationship-building and interpersonal skills in the workplace.

- Consciously strive to be aware of your listeners and how you choose to communicate so that they hear your intended message.

- When you find yourself in the middle of a conflict, address the issues. Use workplace conflicts as an opportunity to use your facilitation skills and understand your coworker's perspective.

- Be specific with your message and your needs. Be brief with your responses and explanations.

Source: Copyright © 2012 by Audrey Nelson and Claire Damken Brown.

Exercise 8.1. A Closing Perspective on Gender Communication

Goal

Review the key points in terms of women's and men's differences in communication behaviors.

Objectives

- Discuss the quotation on slide 8.4 and identify what participants have learned about men's and women's communication styles in the workplace.

- Review participants' perspectives on their next steps.

Timing of Exercise

15 minutes

Materials

Chart paper and easel, markers

Slide 8.4

Setup

☐ In this brief discussion encourage the participants to think about how the quotation relates to what they've learned throughout the program.

☐ Conduct this exercise in dyads and then process it with the entire group, or conduct it in groups of five to eight members, in which each member shares his or her response, and then process it with the entire group.

☐ Ask the participants to read the statement on the slide and then talk with their groups to respond to the two questions.

☐ After three minutes, get the group's attention and ask for a summary from each small group (or from a few sample groups, depending on the audience size).

Slide 8.4

The Gender Times Are Changin'

It used to be axiomatic that girls could cry, but men had to be brave. Only thirty years ago, Edmund Muskie had to abandon his candidacy for the Democratic presidential nomination because he had been brought to a public display of tears. But today a strong woman can be tough, and a strong man can dissolve in emotion. The times, and the genders, they are a-changin'.

—Robin Lakoff, Ph.D. (2010)

1. How does this quote relate to what you have learned about gender communication at today's program?

2. How will you address the gender communication issues you see in your workplace?

Source: Copyright © 2012 by Audrey Nelson and Claire Damken Brown.

Debrief

The facilitator hears from selected groups and writes on the chart the key points raised by the participants. Comments may start with the differences in and acceptance of how men and women express emotions, tears, toughness, strength, and bravery. Hear from the participants how their comments relate to what they have learned throughout the program. In terms of "the times they are a-changin'," discuss with the participants what they will do back in the workplace to ensure that communication between women and men continues to change and improve.

Exercise 8.2. What We've Learned

Goal

Review the program's key points in terms of women's and men's differences in communication behaviors.

Objectives

- Discuss with the participants a summary of what they have learned throughout the program.

- Provide an opportunity for answering the participants' lingering questions.

Timing of Exercise

15 minutes

Materials

Handout: What We've Learned, chart paper and easel, markers

Slide 8.5

Setup

☐ In this closing exercise ask the participants to recall the key points from the discussions held throughout the program.

☐ Process this exercise with the entire group.

☐ Ask the participants to look at the handout and fill in the blanks in the columns under "Women" and "Men."

☐ After the participants have filled in the blanks in the handout, display the slide showing the completed table.

☐ Distribute the handout.

Sample Handout Text: What We've Learned

Fill in the blanks:

Women	Men
Collaborative	
Relationship	Hierarchical, status, authority
Process-oriented	
Ask more questions	Make more commands
	Use more slang and swear words
Discuss feelings and perceptions	
Reply with acknowledgment	Reply with action, to-do's
	Decide quickly
Allowed to express tears	Allowed to express anger
	Hear words
Indirect	

Source: Copyright © 2012 by Audrey Nelson and Claire Damken Brown.

Slide 8.5

What We've Learned

Women	Men
Collaborative	Competitive
Relationship	Hierarchical, status, authority
Process-oriented	Goal-oriented
Ask more questions	Make more commands
Speech is more polite, face-saving	Use more slang and swear words
Discuss feelings and perceptions	Limit emotional content
Reply with acknowledgment	Reply with action, to-do's
Think it over, talk to others	Decide quickly
Allowed to express tears	Allowed to express anger
Hear words and feelings	Hear words
Indirect	Direct

Source: Copyright © 2012 by Audrey Nelson and Claire Damken Brown.

Debrief

Use the closing discussion to review the program's key points. The facilitator may write the answers on a chart as the participants call them out, and then show the slide with the correct responses (completed handout). The facilitator may use this time to answer any other participant questions.

The facilitator decides on the key points that she or he would like listed in the handout and slide. Revise the handout and slide to reflect the key points from the exercises and discussions used throughout the program.

Exercise 8.3. What Men and Women Can Learn from Each Other

Goal

Review the program's key points in terms of code-switching behaviors, an androgynous communication style, and women's and men's communication behaviors.

Objectives

- Discuss with the participants the key communication behaviors that men and women can learn from each other.

- Encourage the participants to use an androgynous communication style moving forward to improve workplace communication between women and men.

Timing of Exercise

10 minutes

Materials

Handout: What Men and Women Can Learn from Each Other, chart paper and easel, markers

Setup

☐ In this closing exercise provide participants with a summary of the communication behaviors they can learn from the opposite sex.

☐ Process this exercise with the entire group.

☐ Ask the participants to review the handout and provide examples of the listed communication behaviors. Depending on the time remaining for the program, ask for examples of only three or four items rather than each item on the chart.

☐ Distribute the handout.

Sample Handout Text: What Men and Women Can Learn from Each Other

Women	Men
Be brief	When listening, look at and face the woman
Be direct	Use supportive verbal and nonverbal messages
Cue the man for the type of listening wanted	Listen versus take action; check whether action is needed
Initiate the conversation	Let others decide the topic of conversation
Communicate your authority more often	Show emotions appropriately
Talk about "I" and accomplishments more often	Allow others to finish their thoughts
Smile when appropriate	Smile more often
Take the floor back; manage interruptions	Interrupt others less frequently

Source: Copyright © 2012 by Audrey Nelson and Claire Damken Brown.

Debrief

As noted in the previous Training Tip, the facilitator may revise the chart in the handout to reflect the key points from the specific exercises and discussions used throughout his or her particular program. The chart is used as a springboard into the facilitator's review of the code-switching and androgynous communication behaviors that were discussed in the program. The facilitator guides the discussion regarding the examples provided by the participants that illustrate the communication behaviors listed in the chart. The number of participants' examples that are discussed depends on the amount of time remaining in the program. It is recommended that the trainers obtain a maximum of three or four examples as illustrations of the program's learning points. Encourage the participants to go forward and use their new knowledge and skills about gender communication styles to support better communication between women and men in the workplace.

> Encourage the participants to go forward and use their new knowledge and skills about gender communication styles to support better communication between women and men in the workplace.

Action Plan and Next Steps

Exercise 8.4. Creating My Next Steps

Goal

Identify the participants' action plans and next steps regarding their enhanced communication skills in their workplace.

Objectives

- Think about the information presented and discussed during the program.

- Identify three next steps.

Timing of Exercise

10 minutes

Materials

Chart paper and easel, markers

Slide 8.6

Setup

☐ Conduct this exercise individually. Ask for volunteers to share their responses, and then process these responses with the entire group.

☐ Ask the participants to read the statement on the slide and then respond to the two questions listed.

☐ Tell the participants they will have a few minutes to write down their next steps. Selected individuals will share their steps with the larger audience.

☐ At three minutes, get the group's attention and ask for a few volunteers to share their next steps with the whole group.

☐ It may be helpful to chart the participants' responses.

Slide 8.6

You must work to create change in the world in which you want to live

Using the information from today's program, identify your three next steps to make your workplace better:

1.

2.

3.
_____

Source: Copyright © 2012 by Audrey Nelson and Claire Damken Brown.

Debrief

Ask for a few volunteers to read their next steps. Encourage all participants to use the skills discussed in the program to create better communication between men and women at work. Thank the group for their participation and questions, and then close the program.

Exercise 8.5. Program Reminders: The Envelope Please!

Goal

Provide program reminders to participants after the completion of the program.

Objectives

- Make time available during the program for participants to write down their program reminders.

- Use the program-reminder process as a facilitator's marketing opportunity four to six weeks after the program has ended.

Timing of Exercise

10 minutes total:

6 minutes: 3 minutes for each designated reflection time during the program

4 minutes at the end of the program to hear a few of the items that the participants wrote down

Materials

Handout: Program Reminders, chart paper and easel, markers, mailing envelopes

Setup

☐ Conduct this exercise individually.

☐ Prepare the handout. Using the facilitator's stationery, state the program's title at the top of the page. Then write, "What did I learn at today's program?" At the bottom of page in the footer area, provide the facilitator's contact information (phone, fax, e-mail address, and mailing address).

☐ Provide a mailing envelope with each handout.

☐ Tell the participants that the list is for their eyes only. No one else will read or see the content except for them. Tell them that at the end of the program they will place the handout in an envelope, seal the envelope, address it, and return it to the facilitator. Four to six weeks after the program, the facilitator will mail the envelopes to the participants. This serves as a reminder to them about the day's discussions and the items they learned.

☐ *Optional:* The facilitator may provide a business card–sized "takeaway card" that is printed on both sides with three bullet points that reflect the program's communication tips. The takeaway card also should contain the facilitator's contact information. Provide one takeaway card per participant. At the end of the program, tell the participants to place the takeaway card in the envelope with their completed list and then seal the envelope.

☐ Tell the participants that there will be two designated times during the program where the facilitator will stop and allow time for them to reflect and add a reminder to the list. Participants may also add items on their own during the program when they hear a particular item that affects them or an item that they want to make certain they remember. The handout has numbered spaces for five reminders; however, the participants may write down additional items as needed.

☐ After the midmorning break, ask the participants to pull out this handout. Tell them they have three minutes to write down a reminder or learning point from the program thus far. The facilitator remains quiet during this reflection time.

☐ At the end of the program, ask the participants to take this handout and use the next three minutes to write down a reminder or learning point from the program. The facilitator remains quiet during this reflection time.

☐ After the participants have written down all five items, tell them to place the handout (and optional takeaway card) in the envelope and seal it.

☐ Ask the participants to address the envelopes to themselves.

☐ Ask the participants to share with the group five different reminders or items they learned during the program. Participants then share their five items.

☐ Collect the sealed, addressed envelopes.

☐ Place the postage on the envelopes and mail them four to six weeks after the program has been completed.

☐ The cost of the stationery, takeaway cards, and stamps should be factored into the pricing of the seminars. The number of participants in the session and related stationery and postage costs may determine whether or not the facilitator uses this particular exercise.

Sample Handout Text: Program Reminders

Gender Communication Training Seminar

What did I learn at today's program?

1.

2.

3.

4.

5.

training tip

The handout example for this exercise states at the top of the page, "What did I learn at today's program?" The facilitator may choose to change this to say something else, such as "Based on today's program, list five action steps to implement back at the office," or "What key points from today's program affected me the most?"

Debrief

The Program Reminders exercise encourages the participants to select which discussions had the greatest impact or what key points had particular meaning for them. Remember that men are not being asked to stop being men; likewise, women are not being asked to stop being women. By sharing some of their program reminders, all of the participants benefit from hearing what others thought was important about the training. This process shows participants acting as role models for the other participants as they share their reminders and talk about how they can improve communication between women and men at the workplace.

Remember, men are not being asked to stop being men; likewise, women are not being asked to stop being women.

The exercise is also a marketing opportunity for the facilitator. The envelope and letter should contain the facilitator's contact information. If the facilitator chooses to use the takeaway card, then the card is also a marketing tool and should list the facilitator's contact information along with a few key points from the program.

At the close of the program, the facilitator or hosts of the training session may have an evaluation form to use to gather participants' program comments. There are a variety of program evaluation forms, and the facilitator can select and design a form for his or her use. See the Additional Instruments and Training Tools section for Chapter Eight for an example evaluation form.

CHAPTER 9

Example One-Hour Program

Men and women need to know direct and indirect methods of influence, and they need to be able to adapt quickly and easily to differences in the person they're trying to influence. An adaptive, flexible stance to understanding and influence is clearly more advantageous than a fixed, oppositional stance.

—Judith Tingley (1994, p. 14)

Learning Objectives

- Suggest content for a one-hour program.
- Provide example agendas of one-hour programs.

Introduction

This chapter provides two example programs. The facilitator may select either program or choose other discussions and exercises from previous chapters to form alternate one-hour programs. Once the facilitator has decided on the focus or theme for the program, she or he may then review the units for suitable key points that support that theme. Themes may address creating workplace change; using code switching and an androgynous communication style; general communication style differences between men and women; men's and women's nonverbal communication differences; men's and women's verbal communication differences; increasing communication tools and skills; improving workplace communication; and so on.

Timing for Example Programs

60 minutes

Materials

Refer to past chapters for materials (handouts, slides, and chart paper and easel) needed for the exercises and discussions recommended in this chapter

Slides 9.1 through 9.4

Example 1: Conquering Conversational Collisions Between Men and Women

This one-hour program's theme is about improving communication between men and women by using code switching and an androgynous communication style (see Table 9.1).

Table 9.1. Example Program 1

Activity	Time	Process	Handout/Slide
A. Introduction			
1. Program title and objectives; workplace benefits for improving gender communication	5 minutes	See the discussion after slides 1.3 and 1.4 in Chapter One.	Slide 9.1 Slide 9.2
2. Seven most-asked questions	20 minutes	Exercise 1.1	Slide 1.1
B. Concepts			
1. Define *code switching*.	5 minutes	See the definition and discussion after slides 1.3 and 1.4 in Chapter One.	Slide 1.5
2. Define *androgynous communication style*.	5 minutes	See the definition and discussion after slides 1.3 and 1.4 in Chapter One.	Slide 1.4
C. Code-switching or androgynous communication-style examples			
1. Pyramid style	5 minutes	See the discussion after slide 5.6 in Chapter Five and after slide 2.4 in Chapter Two.	
2. Sample tips for men and women	10 minutes	See Exercise 8.3 and the table, "What Men and Women Can Learn from Each Other." Select two items for men and two items for women for discussion here.	Create a slide listing the items selected.

Source: Copyright © 2012 by Audrey Nelson and Claire Damken Brown.

Table 9.1. (*continued*)

Activity	Time	Process	Handout/Slide
D. Closing			
1. Summary/final thoughts	5 minutes		Slide 8.2
2. Close the program. Complete the evaluations.	5 minutes	See the Additional Instruments and Training Tools section for the evaluation form.	Evaluation form

Source: Copyright © 2012 by Audrey Nelson and Claire Damken Brown.

Slide 9.1

Conquering Conversational Collisions Between Men and Women

Source: Copyright © 2012 by Audrey Nelson and Claire Damken Brown.

---

training tip

The facilitator may create additional slides to complete the program. For example, the facilitator may add the following slides: program title, objectives, or additional content slides, and end with a slide showing facilitator contact information.

Slide 9.2
Objectives

- Give Me the Bottom Line! He Speaks, She Speaks

- Define Code Switching and an Androgynous Communication Style

- Explore Code-Switching Communication Examples and Tips

- Build Your Communication Tool Kit!

Source: Copyright © 2012 by Audrey Nelson and Claire Damken Brown.

Example 2: Talk Remedies for Communication Between Men and Women

This one-hour program's theme addresses a few communication basics creating awareness for improving interactions between men and women at work (see Table 9.2).

Table 9.2. Example Program 2

Activity	Time	Process	Handout/Slide
A. Introduction			
1. Program title and objectives; workplace benefits for improving gender communication	5 minutes	See the discussion after slides 1.3 and 1.4 in Chapter One.	Slide 9.3 Slide 9.4

Source: Copyright © 2012 by Audrey Nelson and Claire Damken Brown.

Table 9.2. (*continued*)

Activity	Time	Process	Handout/Slide
2. One Thing I Wish the Opposite Sex Would Change in Their Communication Style	12 minutes	Exercise 1.3	Colored paper, slide 1.2

B. Concepts

1. Define *sex* in terms of "sex of communicator."	3 minutes	See Chapter One, "Introduction," for a definition and discussion.	
2. Define *gender* in terms of "gender communication."	5 minutes	See Chapter One, "Introduction," for a definition and discussion.	

C. Discuss Communication Basics

Talk the Talk: Facts and Fiction About Sex Differences in Speech Communication	25 minutes	Exercise 2.1	Handout: "Talk the Talk: Facts and Fiction About Sex Differences in Speech Communication," Slide 2.1

D. Closing

1. Summary/final thoughts	5 minutes		Slide 8.1
2. Close the program. Complete the evaluations.	5 minutes	See the Additional Instruments and Training Tools section for the evaluation form.	Evaluation form

Source: Copyright © 2012 by Audrey Nelson and Claire Damken Brown.

Slide 9.3

Talk Remedies for Communication Between Men and Women

Source: Copyright © 2012 by Audrey Nelson and Claire Damken Brown.

Slide 9.4

Objectives

• Give Me the Bottom Line! He Speaks, She Speaks

• Explore Communication Style Differences

• Take Charge! Improve How Women and Men Communicate

Source: Copyright © 2012 by Audrey Nelson and Claire Damken Brown.

training tip

The facilitator may want a handout for the one-hour program. In the above example program, a handout with the true or false statements (Exercise 2.1) is helpful for discussion purposes. The facilitator may choose to add the following to the handout: program title, facilitator's short bio, objectives, additional content (definitions and key points), recommended resources, and references. End the handout with the facilitator's contact information. Note that in case the handout pages get separated, it is helpful to have the facilitator's contact information on each page.

CHAPTER 10

A Half-Day Program

The only way to grow in our understanding of gender communication is to stretch ourselves to experience a broad range of ways that people enact gender. By developing an open-mindedness to gender beliefs and practices that may be different from our own, we will no longer be limited by our own social positions or viewpoints. By investigating any inequities we discover, we may also become more sensitive to the daily realities some of us face, and help bring about changes that restore fairness and equity.
—*Teri Kwal Gamble and Michael W. Gamble (2003, p. 1)*

Learning Objectives

- Suggest content for a half-day program.
- Provide example agendas for two half-day programs.

Introduction

This chapter provides two example half-day programs. The facilitator may select either program or choose other discussions and exercises from previous chapters to form alternative half-day programs. The length of a half-day program is considered to be three hours long, for example, 9:00 AM to 12:00 PM or 1:00 PM to 4:00 PM. Depending on the program's requirements, facilitators may add exercises and discussions to extend the program to four hours. One ten-minute break is scheduled approximately halfway through the program and is included in the three hours. Depending on the number of participants, adjust the break time accordingly. A fifteen-minute break may be more appropriate if the audience is a large group (forty or more participants). As with the previous program in Chapter Nine, it is recommended that the facilitator first determine the focus or theme for the seminar, and then review the chapters and exercises that support the selected theme.

Timing for Example Programs

3 hours

Materials for Unit

Refer to previous chapters for materials (handouts, slides, and chart paper and easel) needed for the exercises and discussions recommended in this chapter

Slides 10.1 and 10.2

Example 1: Conquering Conversational Collisions Between Men and Women

This half-day program's theme is about improving communication between men and women by using code switching and an androgynous communication style (see Table 10.1).

Table 10.1. Example Program 1

Activity	Time	Process	Handout/Slide
A. Introduction			
1. Program Title and Objectives	5 minutes		Slide 9.1 Slide 10.2
2. The Seven Most-Asked Questions	20 minutes	Exercise 1.1 The slide content is the same as the handout.	Slide 1.1 Handout: The Seven Most-Asked Questions
B. Understanding terms			
1. Define *androgynous communication style.*	5 minutes	See the definition and discussion in the Exercise 1.4 debrief.	Slide 1.4
2. Define *code switching* and *workplace benefits for men and women* using code switching and an androgynous communication style.	5 minutes	See the definition and discussion after slide 1.4.	Slide 1.5
C. Building a communication tool kit: Use code switching and an androgynous communication style			
1. Pyramid Style	5 minutes	See the discussion after slide 5.6 in Chapter Five and after slide 2.4 in Chapter Two.	
2. Talk the Talk: Myths About Sex Differences in Speech Communication	30 minutes	Exercise 2.1 The slide content is the same as the handout. You may display the slide during the handout completion and discussion.	Slide 2.1 Handout: Talk the Talk: Myths About Sex Differences in Speech Communication

Source: Copyright © 2012 by Audrey Nelson and Claire Damken Brown.

Table 10.1. (*continued*)

Activity	Time	Process	Handout/Slide
Action Steps	5 minutes	See slide 2.8 and slide 2.9. Select the action steps you have discussed and create a new slide.	Create a slide listing the selected action steps for men and women.
Break	10–15 minutes		
3. How Men and Women Listen	25 minutes	Exercise 5.5	Handout: How Men and Women Listen
Action Steps	5 minutes	See slide 5.9 and slide 5.10. Select the action steps you have discussed and create a new slide.	Create a slide listing the selected action steps for men and women.
4. Unspoken Messages: Examples of Nonverbal Communication	5 minutes	See the discussion in Exercise 4.1 that addresses slide 4.2 and nonverbal examples.	Slide 4.2
5. Double Messages	15 minutes	Exercise 4.2 First provide the handout. During the debrief of the handout, display and discuss the slide.	Handout: The Impact of Double Messages Slide 4.3
6. First Impressions	15 minutes	Exercise 4.7	Slide 4.6
7. Space Rules, Power, and Status	15 minutes	Exercise 4.8 First distribute the handout. During the debrief of the handout, display and discuss the slide.	Handout: Space Rules, Power, and Status Slide 4.7

Source: Copyright © 2012 by Audrey Nelson and Claire Damken Brown.

Table 10.1. (*continued*)

Activity	Time	Process	Handout/Slide
Action Steps	5 minutes	See slide 4.10 and slide 4.11. Select the action steps you have discussed and create a new slide.	Create a slide listing the selected action steps for men and women.

D. Summary of the half-day's program and closing

Activity	Time	Process	Handout/Slide
1. Summary: Change for the Better	5 minutes	See the Chapter Eight discussion for slide 8.3.	Slide 8.3
2. Creating My Next Steps; close program. Complete and collect the evaluations.	5 minutes	Exercise 8.4 See the Additional Instruments and Training Tools section for the evaluation form.	Slide 8.6 Handout: evaluation form

Source: Copyright © 2012 by Audrey Nelson and Claire Damken Brown.

Slide 10.1

Objectives

- Give Me the Bottom Line! He Speaks, She Speaks

- How She and He Listen

- Strategize Your Unspoken Messages

- Build Your Tool Kit: Code Switching and an Androgynous Communication Style

Source: Copyright © 2012 by Audrey Nelson and Claire Damken Brown.

As mentioned in the previous chapter, the facilitator may create
additional slides to complete her or his program. For example, the
facilitator may end with a slide showing the facilitator contact
information. The handout and slides may include a list of references
and resources or suggested readings; show the facilitator's name,
e-mail address, or other contact information on each handout page.

Example 2: Talk Remedies for Communication Between Men and Women

This half-day program's theme addresses a few communication basics
creating awareness for improving interactions between men and
women at work (see Table 10.2).

Table 10.2. Example Program 2

Activity	Time	Process	Handout/Slide
A. Introduction			
1. Program Title and Objectives	5 minutes		Slides 9.3 and 10.2
2. Workplace Benefits for Improving Gender Communication	5 minutes	See the discussion after slide 1.3 and slide 1.4 in Chapter One.	Create a slide of your key points.
3. One Thing I Wish the Opposite Sex Would Change in Their Communication Style	15 minutes	Exercise 1.3	Colored paper, slide 1.2
B. Understanding terms			
1. Define *sex* in terms of "sex of communicator"; define *gender* in terms of "gender communication."	5 minutes	See the Introduction in Chapter One for definitions and discussions.	

Source: Copyright © 2012 by Audrey Nelson and Claire Damken Brown.

Table 10.2. (*continued*)

Activity	Time	Process	Handout/Slide
2. Define *androgynous communication style.*	5 minutes	See the definition and discussion in the Exercise 1.4 debrief.	Slide 1.4
3. Define *code switching* and *workplace benefits* for men and women using code switching and an androgynous communication style.	5 minutes	See the definition and discussion after slide 1.4.	Slide 1.5

C. Understanding communication-style differences and building skills

Activity	Time	Process	Handout/Slide
1. Talk the Talk: Myths About Sex Differences in Speech Communication	25 minutes	Exercise 2.1 The slide content is the same as the handout. You may display the slide during the handout completion and discussion.	Slide 2.1 Handout: Talk the Talk: Myths About Sex Differences in Speech Communication
2. Pyramid Style	5 minutes	See the discussion after slide 5.6 in Chapter Five and after slide 2.4 in Chapter Two.	
3. Discussion of Tag Questions	5 minutes	See discussion after slide 2.5.	Slide 2.5
Break	10–15 minutes		
Action Steps	5 minutes	See slide 2.8 and slide 2.9. Select the action steps you have discussed and create a new slide.	Create a slide listing the selected action steps for men and women.

Source: Copyright © 2012 by Audrey Nelson and Claire Damken Brown.

Table 10.2. (*continued*)

Activity	Time	Process	Handout/Slide
4. Listening for the Process and Details; Cueing Technique	20 minutes	Exercise 5.8 Include the discussion in Exercise 5.8 debrief that addresses slide 5.7, slide 5.8.	Handout: Case Study: "Get to the Point!" Slides 5.7 and 5.8
Action Steps	5 minutes	See slide 5.9 and slide 5.10. Select the action steps you have discussed and create a new slide.	Create a slide listing the selected action steps for men and women.
5. Unspoken Messages: Examples of Nonverbal Communication	5 minutes	See the discussion in Exercise 4.1 that addresses slide 4.2 and nonverbal examples.	Slide 4.2
6. Assigning Meaning and Value to Nonverbal Communication	15 minutes	Exercise 4.4	Handout: Case Study: Something in the Way She Feels
7. Touch, Power, and Perceived Power	20 minutes	Exercise 4.6	Handout: Touch, Power, and Perceived Power
Action Steps	5 minutes	See slide 4.10 and slide 4.11. Select the action steps you have discussed and create a new slide.	Create a slide listing the selected action steps for men and women.

Source: Copyright © 2012 by Audrey Nelson and Claire Damken Brown.

Table 10.2. (*continued*)

Activity	Time	Process	Handout/Slide
D. Summary of the half-day's program and closing			
1. What Men and Women Can Learn from Each Other	10 minutes	Exercise 8.3 See Exercise 8.3 instructions for preparing the handout.	Handout: What Men and Women Can Learn from Each Other
2. Program Reminders: The Envelope Please! Close the program. Complete and collect the evaluations.	10 minutes	Exercise 8.5 See the Additional Instruments and Training Tools section for the evaluation form.	Handout: Program Reminders and mailing envelopes; Handout: evaluation form

Source: Copyright © 2012 by Audrey Nelson and Claire Damken Brown.

Slide 10.2

Objectives

- Give Me the Bottom Line! He Speaks, She Speaks

- How She and He Listen

- Strategize Your Unspoken Messages

- Build Your Tool Kit: Women's and Men's Communication Styles

Source: Copyright © 2012 by Audrey Nelson and Claire Damken Brown.

training tip

The facilitator can monitor her or his program's time to ensure that the timing for each segment is followed. Be prepared to cut or add a segment when needed due to timing. If a discussion runs longer than planned, identify ahead of time which segment may be eliminated. Likewise, if a segment ends sooner than anticipated, be prepared ahead of time for where to add discussion or add an exercise.

These half-day program examples are timed for three hours, including one ten-minute break. Adjust the timing of the program exercises accordingly if the facilitator chooses to have a fifteen-minute break. In general, the content for a half-day program may be adjusted based on the program focus. The facilitator may choose to focus on only two topics for the program, for example, listening and conflict management. As mentioned earlier, once the facilitator has chosen the theme or focus of the program, he or she will be able to select the applicable exercises and discussions.

CHAPTER 11

A Full-Day Program

Language that pits women against men, that over-emphasizes gender differences and ignores similarities just doesn't help advance our culture or edify our lives. . . . The goal is to bridge gaps in understanding between the sexes, to encourage a dialogue about ways that we are similar and different.

— Diana Ivy and Phil Backlund (2004, p. xii)

Learning Objectives

- Suggest content for a full-day program.
- Provide example agendas of full-day programs.

Introduction

Two example programs are provided in this chapter. The facilitator may select either program or choose other discussions and exercises from previous chapters to form alternative full-day programs. The length of a full-day program is considered six hours long: 9:00 AM to 12:00 PM and then 1:00 PM to 4:00 PM. The program is seven hours in length if one includes an hour for lunch. Two 10-minute breaks are included (one is mid-morning and one is mid-afternoon) in the program. Depending on the program requirements, facilitators may add exercises and discussions to extend the program to eight hours. As with the programs in the previous chapters, it is recommended that the facilitator first determine the focus or theme for the seminar, and then review the chapters that support that particular theme.

Timing for Example Programs

6 hours

Materials for Unit

Refer to past chapters for materials (handouts, slides, and chart paper and easel) needed for the exercises and discussions recommended in this chapter

Slides 11.1 and 11.2

training tip

The length of the break can vary depending on the number of people attending the program. If there are ten to twelve people, a ten-minute break should be adequate. If the program has forty to fifty or more participants, then the facilitator may want the group to have fifteen minutes for a break. Note that when the facilitator says ten minutes for a break, participants may take longer. The facilitator needs to monitor the time for the break and start promptly as needed.

Likewise, when planning time for lunch, based on the number of participants, the facilitator may decide whether forty-five minutes or one hour is adequate. Some groups may have lunch catered for the session or opt for a shorter lunchtime in exchange for ending the program a few minutes earlier.

Example 1: Conquering Conversational Collisions Between Men and Women

This full-day program's theme is about improving communication between men and women by using code switching and an androgynous communication style (see Table 11.1).

Table 11.1. Example Program 1

Activity	Time	Process	Handout/Slide
A. Introduction			
1. Program Title and Objectives	5 minutes		Slide 9.1 Slide 11.1
2. The Seven Most-Asked Questions	20 minutes	Exercise 1.1 The slide content is the same as the handout.	Slide 1.1 Handout: The Seven Most-Asked Questions

Table 11.1. (*continued*)

Activity	Time	Process	Handout/Slide
3. Complete the Code-Switching Quotient	20 minutes	Exercise 1.4 Complete the survey and debrief.	Slide 1.3 Handout: Code-Switching Quotient

B. Understanding terms

1. Define *androgynous communication style.*	5 minutes	See the definition and discussion in the Exercise 1.4 debrief.	Slide 1.4
2. Define *code switching* and *workplace benefits for men and women* using code switching and an androgynous communication style.	5 minutes	See the definition and discussion after slide 1.4.	Slide 1.5

C. Building a communication tool kit: Using code switching and an androgynous communication style

1. Pyramid Style	5 minutes	See the discussion after slide 5–6 in Chapter Five and after slide 2.4 in Chapter Two.	
2. Talk the Talk: Myths About Sex Differences in Speech Communication	30 minutes	Exercise 2.1 The slide content is the same as the handout. You may display the slide during the handout completion and discussion.	Slide 2.1 Handout: Talk the Talk: Myths About Sex Differences in Speech Communication

Table 11.1. (*continued*)

Activity	Time	Process	Handout/Slide
Break	10–15 minutes		
Action Steps	5 minutes	See slide 2.8 and slide 2.9. Select the action steps you have discussed and create a new slide.	Create a slide listing the selected action steps for men and women.
3. How Men and Women Listen	25 minutes	Exercise 5.5	Handout: How Men and Women Listen
4. Listening for the Process and Details	20 minutes	Exercise 5.8 Include the discussion in the Exercise 5.8 debrief that addresses slide 5.7 and slide 5.8.	Handout: Case Study: "Get to the point!" Slides 5.7 and 5.8
Action Steps	5 minutes	See slide 5.9 and slide 5.10. Select the action steps you have discussed and create a new slide.	Create a slide listing the selected action steps for men and women.
5. Gender and Emoticons	10 minutes	Exercise 7.1 The slide 7.1 content is the same as the handout. You may display the slide during the handout completion and discussion.	Slide 7.1 Handout: Gender and Emoticons Slides 7.2 and 7.3
6. Gender and E-Mail: Credibility	5 minutes	Exercise 7.2	Slide 7.4
7. Gender and E-Mail: Process Versus Goal	10 minutes	Exercise 7.3	Handout: Case Study: Her Process Format Versus His Goal Format

Table 11.1. (*continued*)

Activity	Time	Process	Handout/Slide
Lunch Break	45 minutes to 1 hour		
Action Steps	5 minutes	See slide 7.8 and slide 7.9. Select the action steps you have discussed and create a new slide.	Create a slide listing the selected action steps for men and women.
8. Unspoken Messages: Can You Not *Not* Communicate? List Nonverbal Behaviors	20 minutes	Exercise 4.1 First provide the handout. During the debrief of the handout, display and discuss both slides.	Handout: Find Meaning in What You Don't Say Slides 4.1 and 4.2
9. Double Messages	15 minutes	Exercise 4.2 First provide the handout. During the debrief of the handout, display and discuss the slide.	Handout: The Impact of Double Messages Slide 4.3
10. Behaviors On or Off the Record	15 minutes	Exercise 4.3	Slide 4.4
11. First Impressions	15 minutes	Exercise 4.7	Slide 4.6
12. Space Rules, Power, and Status	15 minutes	Exercise 4.8 First provide the handout. During the debrief of the handout, display and discuss the slide.	Handout: Space Rules, Power, and Status Slide 4.7
Action Steps	5 minutes	See slides 4.10 and 4.11. Select the action steps you have discussed and create a new slide.	Create a slide listing the selected action steps for men and women.

Table 11.1. (*continued*)

Activity	Time	Process	Handout/Slide
Break	10–15 minutes		
13. Reflection Exercise for Women	20 minutes	Exercise 6.2 First provide the handout. During the debrief of the handout, display and discuss the slides. Slide 6.5 has the same content as the handout.	Handout: Do Women in the Group Resonate with Any of These Themes? Slides 6.4 and 6.5
14. Reflection Exercise for Men	20 minutes	Exercise 6.3	Handout: Do the Men in the Group Resonate with Any of These Themes? Slides 6.6 and 6.7
15. Play Fighting: The Male Banter Game	15 minutes	Exercise 6.5	Slide 6.8 Handout: Case Study: The Male Banter Game
Action Steps	5 minutes	See slides 6.16 and 6.17. Select the action steps you have discussed and create a new slide.	Create a slide listing the selected action steps for men and women.

Table 11.1. (*continued*)

Activity	Time	Process	Handout/Slide
D. Summary of full-day's program and closing			
1. Sample Action Steps for Men and Women	5 minutes	Select items from the action steps mentioned earlier in this program for summary discussion here.	Create a slide listing the selected action steps.
2. Summary: Change for the Better	5 minutes	See the discussion in Chapter Eight for slide 8.3.	Slide 8.3
3. Creating My Next Steps	5 minutes	Exercise 8.4	Slide 8.6
4. Close the program. Complete and collect the evaluations.	5 minutes	See the section on Additional Instruments and Training Tools for the evaluation form.	Handout: evaluation form

The facilitator may create additional slides to complete the program. For example, the facilitator may add additional content slides, references, and resources and end with a slide showing the facilitator contact information.

Slide 11.1
Objectives

- Give Me the Bottom Line! He Speaks, She Speaks

- How She and He Listen

- He and She Wired: The Technology Advantage

- Strategize Your Unspoken Messages: Personal Space and Power

- Recognize Conflict and How to Fight Fair

- Build Your Tool Kit: Code Switching and an Androgynous Communication Style

Source: Copyright © 2012 by Audrey Nelson and Claire Damken Brown.

As mentioned previously, the facilitator may choose to add the following to the handout: program title, facilitator's short bio, objectives, additional content (definitions and key points), recommended resources, and references. Remember to add the facilitator's contact information to each handout page.

Example 2: Talk Remedies for Communication Between Men and Women

This full-day program's theme addresses a few communication basics for improving interactions between men and women at work (see Table 11.2).

Table 11.2. Example Program 2

Activity	Time	Process	Handout/Slide
A. Introduction			
1. Program Title and Objectives	5 minutes		Slide 9.3 Slide 11.2
2. Workplace Benefits for Improving Gender Communication	5 minutes	See the discussion after slide 1.3 and slide 1.4 in Chapter One.	Create a slide of your key points
3. One Thing I wish the Opposite Sex Would Change in Their Communication Style	15 minutes	Exercise 1.3	Colored paper, slide 1.2
B. Understanding terms			
1. Define *sex* in terms of "sex of communicator"; define *gender* in terms of "gender communication."	5 minutes	See the introduction in Chapter One for definitions and discussion.	
2. Define *androgynous communication style.*	5 minutes	See the definition and discussion in the Exercise 1.4 debrief.	Slide 1.4
3. Define *code switching* and *workplace benefits for men and women* using code switching and an androgynous communication style.	5 minutes	See the definition and discussion after slide 1.4.	Slide 1.5

Table 11.2. (*continued*)

Activity	Time	Process	Handout/Slide
C. Understanding communication style differences and building skills			
1. Talk the Talk: Myths About Sex Differences in Speech Communication	25 minutes	Exercise 2.1 The slide content is same as the handout. You may display the slide during the handout completion and discussion.	Slide 2.1 Handout: Talk the Talk: Myths About Sex Differences in Speech Communication
2. Pyramid Style	5 minutes	See the discussion after slide 5.6 in Chapter Five and after slide 2.4 in Chapter Two.	
3. Discussion of Tag Questions	5 minutes	See the discussion after slide 2.5.	Slide 2.5
4. Compare Most Direct to Least Direct: How Do I Ask the Question?	15 minutes	Exercise 2.4	Handout: Compare Most Direct to Least Direct: How Do I Ask the Question? Slide 2.7
Break	10–15 minutes		
Action Steps	5 minutes	See slides 2.8 and 2.9. Select the action steps you have discussed and create a new slide.	Create a slide listing the selected action steps for men and women.

Table 11.2. (*continued*)

Activity	Time	Process	Handout/Slide
5. When He Interrupts Her	20 minutes	Exercise 3.2 In the debrief include discussion of slide 3.1 and definitions for turn taking, overlapping, and interrupting, as mentioned in the first section of Chapter Three.	Handout: Case Study: "Let Me Finish!" Slide 3.1
6. Women's and Men's Perspectives: Other and Self / Me and You	20 minutes	Exercise 3.3	Slide 3.2
Action Steps	5 minutes	See slides 3.3 and 3.4. Select the action steps you have discussed and create a new slide.	Create a slide listing the selected action steps for men and women.
7. Start the Conversation: How She and He Listen	10 minutes	Exercise 5.1	Slide 5.1
8. His and Her Listening Behaviors	20 minutes	Exercise 5.2	Slide 5.2
Lunch Break	45 minutes to 1 hour		
9. Listening for the Process and Details; Cueing Technique	20 minutes	Exercise 5.8 In the Exercise 5.8 debrief include discussion of slides 5.7 and 5.8.	Handout: Case Study: "Get to the Point!" Slides 5.7 and 5.8

Table 11.2. (*continued*)

Activity	Time	Process	Handout/Slide
Action Steps	5 minutes	See slides 5.9 and 5.10. Select the action steps you have discussed and create a new slide.	Create a slide listing the selected action steps for men and women.
10. Find Meaning in What You Don't Say	20 minutes	Exercise 4.1 First provide the handout. During the debrief of the handout, display and discuss both slides.	Handout: Find Meaning in What You Don't Say Slides 4.1 and 4.2
11. Double Messages	15 minutes	Exercise 4.2 First provide the handout. During the debrief of the handout, display and discuss the slide.	Handout: The Impact of Double Messages Slide 4.3
12. Handout: Case Study: Something in the Way She Feels	15 minutes	Exercise 4.4	Handout: Case Study: Something in the Way She Feels
13. Space Invaders: Women or Men?	15 minutes	Exercise 4.8	Slide 4.8
Break	10–15 minutes		
14. Touch, Power, and Perceived Power	20 minutes	Exercise 4.6	Handout: Touch, Power, and Perceived Power
Action Steps	5 minutes	See slides 4.10 and 4.11. Select the action steps you have discussed and create a new slide.	Create a slide listing the selected action steps for men and women.

Table 11.2. (*continued*)

Activity	Time	Process	Handout/Slide
15. Self-Assessment of Childhood Conflict Patterns	15 minutes	Exercise 6.1 The slide 6.1 content is the same as the handout. You may display the slide during the handout completion and discussion. Include slides 6.2 and 6.3.	Handout: Warm-Up Exercise: The Playground as Battleground Slides 6.1, 6.2, and 6.3
16. Men, Women, and Emotional Display	10 minutes	Exercise 6.9	Handout: The Emotional Continuum
Action Steps	5 minutes	See slides 6.16 and 6.17. Select the action steps you have discussed and create a new slide.	Create a slide listing the selected action steps for men and women.

D. Summary of the full-day's program and closing

Activity	Time	Process	Handout/Slide
1. What Men and Women Can Learn from Each Other	10 minutes	Exercise 8.3	Handout: What Men and Women Can Learn from Each Other
2. Program Reminders: The Envelope Please!	10 minutes	Exercise 8.5	Handout: Program Reminders, and mailing envelopes
3. Close the program. Complete and collect the evaluations.	5 minutes	See the Additional Instruments and Training Tools section for the evaluation form.	Handout: evaluation form

Slide 11.2

Objectives

- Give Me the Bottom Line! He Speaks, She Speaks

- How She and He Listen

- Strategize Your Unspoken Messages: Personal Space, Touch, and Power

- Recognize Conflict and Fight Fair

- Enhance Your Awareness of Women's and Men's Communication Styles

Source: Copyright © 2012 by Audrey Nelson and Claire Damken Brown.

The full-day program examples are timed for six hours, including two 10-minute breaks. As mentioned earlier, adjust the timing of the exercises accordingly if the facilitator chooses a longer break time.

ADDITIONAL INSTRUMENTS AND TRAINING TOOLS

Chapter 1: Getting Started: Are Men and Women Just Born Different or Do They Learn to Be Different?

ABC NEWS Productions. (2006, September 9). *The difference between men and women.* 20/20 (transcript only).

Chapter 6: Men, Women, and Conflict: Take It Like a Man Versus Nice Girls Don't Do Conflict

Exercise: Ball Throwing as a Metaphor for Conflict

Goal

Use ball throwing as a metaphor for how men and women handle conflict.

Objectives

- Explore how sex roles affect men's and women's approaches to conflict (throwing the ball easier, harder, and trickier).

- Understand the sex differences in women's and men's comfort level with an increasing intensity of ball throwing.

- Create an awareness of the gender-marked strategies employed when men and women are negotiating for the ball.

Timing of Exercise

10–15 minutes

Materials

Slides, chart paper and easel, markers

Rubber balls approximately the size of tennis balls and in different colors. Each dyad takes a ball. If there is an odd number of participants, make one person an "observer" and include that individual in the debriefing session to share his or her observations.

Setup

☐ Distribute the balls to the tables. One ball per dyad is required.

☐ Ask the participants to stand up, remove all barriers (no tables or chairs between dyads), pick a partner, and stand ten to twelve feet away from and facing their partner.

☐ Each dyad should have one ball. Dyads can be either coed or the same gender.

☐ First, instruct the participants to throw the ball *gently* back and forth. Note that even when the environment is relaxed and we are throwing the ball, some people will drop it or miss catching it.

☐ Second, escalate the intensity. "Now whoever is holding the ball, I want you to throw the ball *harder.*"

☐ Third, escalate the intensity again. "Now whoever is holding the ball, I want you to throw it *trickily.*"

☐ Fourth, and the final command: "Whoever is not holding the ball, walk up to your partner who is holding the ball and get the ball from them. Convince your partner to give it to you."

Debrief

The following are some Dialogue questions for the group. Ask the questions with everyone standing with their partner.

1. First, when you were instructed to throw the ball *gently* back and forth:

   Questions: How did this feel? Relaxed? Fun? *Analysis statement:* Just like conflict, if someone throws something at us in a gentle and relaxed manner, we tend to be more receptive and return the ball in the same fashion. However, even when we attempted to throw the ball in an easy, receptive fashion, some of us still dropped it. Just as with managing conflict, when we are careful and thoughtful in our approach, miscommunications can still occur.

2. Second, when you were instructed to throw the ball *harder* at your partner:

   Questions: How did throwing the ball harder at your partner feel? What were the men thinking when they were instructed to throw it harder? Typical statements from men: "Let me at them." "They are going to get it." What the women were thinking: "I feel uncomfortable." "I don't want to hurt anyone." "I want to go back to throwing the ball nicely." *Analysis statements:* The comfort level among men was acceptable with throwing the ball harder, but the level was low for women. Also, same-sex dyads may have different responses. Male/male dyads report having fun throwing the ball harder (like banter play fighting), and female/female dyads often say they ignored the instructions to throw the ball harder and went back to the first instructions: throw it nicely.

3. Third, when you were instructed to throw the ball *trickily*:

   Questions: Let's hear from the men in the group. There was a lot of creativity and laughing when I said, "Throw the ball trickily." Some of you managed to get the ball stuck in a light fixture. *Analysis statements:* Men became very engaged in the "game" part of throwing the ball trickily, as they often do in conflict. It is "sport." Some men may respond, "How can I confuse them and make it hard?" "Oh yes, now we are having fun!" "I am going to make them work for it."

Questions: Now let's hear from the women in the group. You were also laughing, but groaning when you had to go under or bend over tables to retrieve the ball; maybe this was not a whole lot of fun for the women in the group? Some of you struggled to decide how to throw the ball trickily. *Analysis statements:* Game playing and being tricky may not be as much fun for women as it is for the men in the group. Some women may respond, "I didn't want to make it hard for them" or "I felt bad when she had to chase it." "Why can't we just play nicely?"

4. Finally, what kinds of strategies did you employ to coax the ball from your partner?

The range of strategies and tactics are usually gender-marked. Women will often say, "I just asked nicely, and they gave me the ball" or "I told them how much I would appreciate it if they gave me the ball, and I promised to give it back." Women will usually employ polite strategies. In contrast, some men may report, "I just grabbed it from them" or "I told them they would be in trouble if they did not give up the ball." Men often use banter, threats, or pay the person to give up the ball.

Exercise: Gender and Conflict Style Self-Assessment

Goal

Gender and Conflict Style Self-Assessment

Objectives

- Identify high and low styles of conflict: competition, compromise, collaboration, accommodation, and avoidance.

- Identify whether personal style is characteristically male or female.

- Understand that there can be individual differences in conflict style.

Timing of Exercise

45 minutes to 1 hour

Materials

Slides, chart paper and easel, markers, Thomas-Kilmann Conflict Mode Instrument (TKI) by Kenneth W. Thomas and Ralph H. Kilmann. You can purchase the instruments from:

CPP, Inc.

1055 Joaquin Road, 2nd floor

Mountain View, CA 94043

800–624–1765

https://www.cpp.com/products/tki/index.aspx

Setup

☐ Each participant completes the Thomas-Kilmann Conflict Mode Instrument (TKI).

☐ Participants identify "high" use styles (a score of 9–12) and "low" use styles (0–4).

☐ Participants identify their highest score (the style they use the most) and are segregated into five groups representing each of the styles: competition, compromise, collaboration, accommodation, and avoidance. For example, all high competitors are in one group, high avoiders are in another group, and so on. The groups sit in a circle or at individual tables.

Debrief

1. The profile of the TKI scores indicates the repertoire of conflict-handling modes. It assesses individuals on five styles that can be

linked to male and female styles. The general descriptions of these styles are found in the TKI:

- *Competing* is assertive and uncooperative—an individual pursues his or her own concerns at the other person's expense. This is a power-oriented mode in which you use whatever power seems appropriate to win your own position—your ability to argue, your rank or economic sanctions. Competing means standing up for your rights, defending a position which you believe is correct, or simply trying to win.

- *Collaboration* is moderate in both assertiveness and cooperativeness. The objective is to find some expedient, mutually acceptable solution that partially satisfies both parties. It falls intermediate between competing and accommodating.

- *Compromising* is moderate in both assertiveness and cooperativeness. The objective is to find some expedient, mutually acceptable solution that partially satisfies both parties. It falls intermediate between competing and accommodating. Compromising might mean splitting the difference between the two positions, exchanging concessions or seeking a quick middle-ground solution.

- *Avoiding* is unassertive and uncooperative—the person neither pursues his or her own concerns nor those of the other individual. They do not deal with the conflict. Avoiding might take the form of diplomatically sidestepping an issue, postponing an issue until a better time or simply withdrawing from a threatening situation.

- *Accommodating* is unassertive and cooperative—the complete opposite of competing. When accommodating, the individual neglects his or her own concerns to satisfy the concerns of the other person; there is an element of self-sacrifice in this mode.

Accommodating might take the form of selfless generosity or charity, obeying another person's order when you would prefer not to or yielding to another's point of view [Thomas & Kilmann, 2007].

Generally, high competitors will be men. Refer to the description of the competition style. The characteristics are typically a male orientation to conflict: power-oriented and trying to win.

In contrast, high avoiders and accommodators will be women. Refer to the characteristics of accommodation: neglects their concerns to satisfy the concerns of others, and yielding to another person. Avoidance is also typically a female orientation to conflict: neglects their personal needs to satisfy the needs of the other person, withdrawing from a threatening situation and not dealing with the conflict.

2. Ask the groups to discuss any gender-marked connections they perceive with their high style; for example, the number of women in the accommodation or avoidance groups and the number of men in the competition groups.

3. There will be counterintuitive members in the various groups; for example, a man with a high avoidance style or a woman with a high competition style. Ask them to explore why they think they employ those styles. Responses may include situational concerns and adaptations. From a man with a high avoidance style: "If you had my boss, you have to avoid conflict. He has to be the winner." Recall the point made in the training that men will compete but avoid it if they think they cannot win. From a woman with a high competition style: "I am a litigator, and the nature of my profession requires me to be competitive and aggressive."

4. Probing questions: Would we expect more women to avoid and accommodate? Would we expect more men to compete? Are the compromise and collaboration styles gender-marked? Why or why not? Does this group represent typical gender conflict styles?

Chapter 8: Final Thoughts on Reaching Across the Gender Divide

Example

EVALUATION FORM

How would you rate this presentation overall? (circle one)

1	2	3	4	5
Excellent	Very Good	Good	Average	Poor

The ideas presented were: (circle one)

1	2	3	4	5
Excellent	Very Good	Good	Average	Poor

Would you attend another presentation given by this presenter? (circle one)

Yes or No

If you answered yes, what other topics would you like this presenter to address?

What I liked best:

What I would have changed:

Additional comments:

Name (optional) _____

RECOMMENDED RESOURCES

Chapter 1: Getting Started: Are Men and Women Just Born Different or Did They Learn to Be Different?

Sargent, A. (1983). *The androgynous manager*. New York, NY: AMACOM.

Chapter 2: He Speaks, She Speaks: What Different Things They Say

McCornack, S. (2007). *Reflect and relate: An introduction to interpersonal communication*. New York, NY: Bedford/St. Martin's.

Chapter 3: Gender Conversation Technicalities: Interruptions, Overlapping, and Other Turn-Taking Dilemmas

Holmes, J., & Meyerhoff, M. (Eds.). (2003). *The handbook of language and gender*. Malden, MA: Blackwell Publishing.

Chapter 4: Women, Men, and Unspoken Messages

Andersen, P. (2004). *The complete idiot's guide to body language*. New York, NY: Penguin.

Eakins, B. W., & Eakins, R. G. (1978). *Sex differences in human communication*. Boston, MA: Houghton Mifflin.

Gladwell, M. (2005). *Blink: The power of thinking without thinking*. New York, NY: Little, Brown and Company.

Hall, E. T. (1973). *The silent language*. Garden City, NY: Anchor Books.

Chapter 5: How She and He Listen

Mindell, P. (2001). *How to say it for women*. New York, NY: Prentice Hall.

Chapter 6: Men, Women, and Conflict: Take It Like a Man Versus Nice Girls Don't Do Conflict

Runde, C. E., & Flanagan, T. A. (2010). *Developing your conflict competence: A hands-on guide for leaders, managers, facilitators, and teams*. San Francisco, CA: Jossey-Bass.

Wilmont, W., & Hocker, J. (1998). *Interpersonal conflict* (5th ed.). Boston, MA: McGraw-Hill.

Chapter 7: He and She Wired

Chan, J. F. (2008). *E-mail: A write it well guide: How to write and manage e-mail in the workplace*. Oakland, CA: Write It Well.

Chapter 8: Final Thoughts on Reaching Across the Gender Divide

Dow, B. J., & Wood, J. T. (Eds.). (2006). *The Sage handbook of gender and communication*. Thousand Oaks, CA: Sage.

Helgesen, S. (1990). *The female advantage: Women's ways of leadership*. New York, NY: Doubleday.

Chapter 9: Example One-Hour Program

Canary, D., & Dindia, K. (Eds.). (1998). *Sex differences and similarities in communication*. Mahwah, NJ: Erlbaum.

Chapter 10: A Half-Day Program

Babcock, L., & Laschever, S. (2003). *Women don't ask: Negotiation and the gender divide*. Princeton, NJ: Princeton University Press.

Helgesen, S. (1995). *The web of inclusion*. New York, NY: Currency Doubleday.

Chapter 11: A Full-Day Program

Gurian, M. (with Annis, B.). (2008). *Leadership and the sexes: Using gender science to create success in business*. San Francisco, CA: Jossey-Bass.

REFERENCES

Baron, N. S. (2004). See you online: Gender issues in college student use of instant messaging. *Journal of Language and Social Psychology, 23*(4), 397–423.

Bate, B. (1992). *Communication and the sexes.* Prospect Heights, IL: Waveland Press.

Bloom, A. (2002, October). Why can't a woman be more like a man? And vice versa? *O, The Oprah Magazine, 3*(10), 67.

Borisoff, D., & Merrill, L. (1992). *The power to communicate: Gender differences as barriers.* (2nd ed.). Prospect Heights, IL: Waveland Press.

Boutin, C. (2006, August 22). Snap judgments decide a face's character, psychologist finds. Retrieved from http://www.princeton.edu /main/news/archive/S15/62/69K40/index.xml?section=topstories

Brajer, V., & Gill, A. (2010). Yakity-yak: Who talks back? An e-mail experiment. *Social Science Quarterly, 91,* 1007–1024.

Brescoll, V. (2007). How to walk the tightrope of "nice and able": Overcoming workplace challenges for female bosses. *Psychology of Women Quarterly, 31*(2), 217–218. doi:10.1111/j.1471-6402.2007.00354_2.x

Brescoll, V., & Okimoto, T. (2010). The price of power: Power-seeking and backlash against female politicians. *Personality and Social Psychology Bulletin, 36*(7), 923–936.

Brescoll, V., & Uhlmann, E. L. (2008). Can an angry woman get ahead? Gender, status conferral, and workplace emotion expression. *Psychological Science, 19*(3), 268–275.

Brown, C., & Nelson, A. (2009). *Code switching: How to talk so men will listen.* New York, NY: Alpha Books.

Brown, N. (2001). Edward T. Hall: Proxemic theory, 1966. Santa Barbara: Regents of the University of California. Retrieved from http://www .csiss.org/classics/content/13

Brown, P., & Levinson, S. (1978). Universals in language usage: Politeness phenomena. In E. Goody, *Questions and politeness: Strategies in social interaction.* Cambridge, UK: Cambridge University Press.

Brown, S. (1999). Handshake intimidation. Grass Valley, CA: Shamus Brown. Retrieved from http://sales-tips.industrialego.com/sales-articles /feb1201.htm

Colley, A., & Todd, Z. (2002). Gender-linked differences in the style and content of e-mails to friends. *Journal of Language and Social Psychology, 21*(4), 380–392.

Conniff, R. (2004, January). Reading faces. *Smithsonian, 34*(10), 44–50.

Cox, D. (2000, January). Comparison of anger expression in men and women reveals surprising differences. *Science Daily.* Retrieved from http:// www.sciencedaily.com/releases/2000/01/000131075609.htm

Deveny, K. (1994, December 5). Chart of kindergarten awards. *Wall Street Journal,* p. B1.

Eakins, B., & Eakins, G. (1978). *Sex differences in human communication.* Boston, MA: Houghton Mifflin.

Gamble, T. K., & Gamble, M. W. (2003). *The gender communication connection.* Boston, MA: Houghton Mifflin.

Gilligan, C. (1982). *In a different voice: Psychological theory and women's development.* Cambridge, MA: Harvard University Press.

Glass, L. (1993). *He says, she says: Closing the communication gap between the sexes.* New York, NY: Pedigree.

Herring, S. C. (1994, June). *Gender differences in computer-mediated communication: Bringing familiar baggage to the new frontier.* Keynote address at the American Library Association Annual Convention, Miami, Florida.

Herring, S. C. (2003). Gender and power in online communication. In J. Holmes & M. Meyerhoff (Eds.), *The handbook of language and gender* (pp. 202–228). Oxford, UK: Blackwell Publishers.

Hess, L., & Atkins, M. (1998). Victims and aggressors at school: Teacher, self, and peer perceptions of psychosocial functioning. *Applied Developmental Science, 2*(2), 75–89.

Horng, E. (2007, April 7). *No-e-mail fridays transform office.* Retrieved from http://abcnews.go.com

Ivy, D., & Backlund, P. (2004). *GenderSpeak: Personal effectiveness in gender communication* (3rd ed.). New York, NY: McGraw-Hill.

Johnston, M. K., Weaver, J., Watson, K., & Barker, L. (2000). Listening styles: Biological or psychological differences? *International Journal of Listening, 14,* 32–47.

Jones, S. (1986). Sex differences in touch communication. *The Western Journal of Communication, 50*(Summer), 227–241.

Jung, C. G., Shamdasani, S., Kyburz, M., & Peck, J. (2009). *The red book.* London, England: W. W. Norton.

Katsuno, H., & Yano, C. (2007). Kaomoji and expressivity in a Japanese housewives' chatroom. In B. Danet & S. C. Herring (Eds.), *The multilingual internet: Language, culture, and communication online* (pp. 278–301). New York, NY: Oxford University Press.

Kenrick, D. T., Neuberg, S. L., & Cialdini, R. B. (2002). *Social psychology: Unraveling the mystery* (2nd ed.). Boston, MA: Allyn & Bacon.

Kreamer, A., & Thompson, W. (2011). *It's always personal: Emotion in the new workplace.* New York, NY: Random House.

Krohn, F. (2004). A generational approach to using emoticons as non-verbal communication. *Journal of Technical Writing and Communication, 34*(4), 321–328.

Lakoff, R. (1975). *Language and woman's place.* New York, NY: Harper Torch Books.

Lakoff, R. (1990a). Extract from language and woman's place. In D. Cameron (Ed.), *The feminist critique of language: A reader* (pp. 221–233). London, England: Routledge.

Lakoff, R. (1990b). *Talking power: The politics of language.* New York, NY: Basic Books.

Lakoff, R. (2010, November 7). Election 2010: Man pants and the girlie-man. Retrieved from http://www.huffingtonpost.com/robin-lakoff /election-2010-the-man-pan_b_780113.html

Mair, V. H. (2009, September). *Danger + opportunity ≠ equal crisis: How a misunderstanding about Chinese characters has led many astray.* Retrieved from http://pinyin.info/chinese/crisis.html

Making a great first impression. (n.d.). Retrieved from http://www.mindtools .com/CommSkll/FirstImpressions.html

Mayo, C., & Henley, N. M. (1981). *Gender and nonverbal behavior.* New York, NY: Springer-Verlag.

Mehrabian, A. (1981). *Silent messages: Implicit communication of emotion and attitudes* (2nd ed.). Belmont, CA: Wadsworth.

Mencken, H. L. (1920). *In defense of women.* New York, NY: Alfred A. Knopf. Retrieved from http://www.brainyquote.com/quotes/authors /h/h_l_mencken_4.html

Mendell, A. (1996). *How men think: The seven essential rules for making it in a man's world.* New York, NY: Ballantine.

Mindell, P. (1995). *A women's guide to the language of success: Communicating with confidence and power.* Englewood Cliffs, NJ: Prentice Hall.

Nelson, A. (with Golant, S.). (2004). *You don't say: Navigating nonverbal communication between the sexes.* New York, NY: Prentice Hall.

Payne, K. (2001). *Different but equal.* Westport, CT: Praeger.

Pearson, J. (1985). *Gender and Communication.* Dubuque, IA: William C. Brown.

Phillips, L., & Ferguson, A. (2004). *Women seen and heard: Lessons learned from successful speakers.* Santa Barbara, CA: Luz Publications.

Richmond, V. P., McCroskey, J., & Payne, S. (1991). *Nonverbal behavior in interpersonal relations.* Englewood Cliffs, NJ: Prentice Hall.

Rubin. H. (1998). *The princessa: Machiavelli for women.* New York, NY: Random House.

Sargent, S. L., & Weaver, J. (2003). Listening styles: Sex differences in perceptions of self and others. *International Journal of Listening, 17*(1), 5–18.

Tannen, D. (1990). *You just don't understand: Women and men in conversation.* New York, NY: William Morrow.

Tannen, D. (1994). *Talking from 9 to 5: How women's and men's conversational styles affect who gets heard, who gets credit and what gets done at work.* New York, NY: William Morrow.

Thomas, K. W., & Kilmann, R. H. (2007). *Thomas-Kilmann Conflict Mode Instrument* (TKI). Mountain View, CA: CPP, Inc.

Tingley, J. (1994). *Genderflex: Men and women speaking each other's language at work.* New York, NY: AMACOM.

West, C. (1998). When the doctor is a "lady": Power, status and gender in physician-patient encounters. In J. Coates (Ed.), *Language and gender: A reader* (pp. 396–412). Malden, MA: Blackwell Publishing.

West, C., & Zimmerman, D. (1998). Women's place in everyday talk: Reflections on parent-child interaction. Revised version of paper presented at American Sociological Association Annual Meetings, August 25–30, 1975, San Francisco, CA. In J. Coates (Ed.), *Language and gender: A reader* (pp. 166–175). Malden, MA: Blackwell Publishing.

Willis, J., & Todorov, A. (2006). First impressions: Making up your mind after a 100-ms exposure to a face. *Psychological Science, 17*(7), 592–598.

Witmer, D., & Katzman, S. (1997). On-line smiles: Does gender make a difference in the use of graphic accents? *Journal of Computer Mediated Communication, 2*(4). Retrieved from http://jcmc.indiana.edu/vol2/issue4/witmer1.html

Wolf, A. (2000). Emotional expression online: Gender differences in emoticon use. *CyberPsychology and Behavior, 3*(5), 827–833.

Wood, J. (1998). *But I thought you meant . . . Misunderstandings in human communication.* Mountain View, CA: Mayfield.

Wood, J. (2005). *Gendered lives: Communication, gender and culture* (6th ed.). Belmont, CA: Wadsworth.

Zimmerman, D., & West, C. (1975). Sex roles, interruptions, and silences in conversations. In B. Thorne & N. Henley (Eds.), *Language and sex: Difference and dominance* (pp. 105–129). Rowley, MA: Newbury House.

INDEX

Page references followed by *t* indicate a table.

A

Accommodating style, 302–303

Action steps for men: for changing nonverbal behaviors, 132; for changing speech for, 62; identifying participants' next steps for, 256–257; for improving conflict resolution, 215; for improving e-mail communication, 239; for improving listening skills, 169

Action steps for women: for changing nonverbal behaviors, 133; for changing speech, 63; identifying participants' next steps for, 256–257; for improving conflict resolution, 216; for improving e-mail communication, 240; for improving listening skills, 170; when you are interrupted or overlapped, 86

Addington, D.W., 131

Aggressive behavior: credibility built through, 212; female rejected by peers over, 177; male bantering and, 176–179. *See also* Conflict

Androgynous gender communication: appreciating the value of, 60–63; characteristics of, 26–28; The Code-Switching Quotient on, 23–25; creating more equitable workplace using, 245–248; full-day training program on, 283–289; half-day training program on, 272–276; one-hour training program on, 264–267. *See also* Code switching; Communication styles; Gender communication skills

Androgyny concept: code switching ability of, 26; communication characteristics of, 26–28; definition of, 25

Anger: confers more status for men, 204–205; crying as expression of female, 208; double standard in expressing, 202–205; female passive-aggressive behavior response to, 197–200; female suppression and male expression of, 196–197; gender role in flight or fight response, 194–197; men feel less effective when forced to hold in, 203; status level and gender expression of, 205; women experience a backlash when they express, 204. *See also* Emotions

Anima and animus, 26

Apologies: female tendency toward making more, 46, 47; men use less emotion during, 47

Appropriate touching, 102

Artifacts: description of, 90; nonverbal communication using, 90

Atkins, M., 177

Avoidance: as male response to emotions, 209–211; Thomas-Kilmann Conflict Mode Instrument (TKI) scores on, 211, 302

313

INDEX **325**

exhibited during conflict, 187; female process-oriented and male goal-oriented, 54–57; female use of indirect verb forms, 46; how men present direct comments and feedback, 51–53; male use of adjectives and adverbs, 39, 42; male use of declarative sentences, 39, 42–43; most direct to least direct way to ask questions, 58–60; women presenting comment embedded in questions, 48–50. *See also* Language

"Split-ear phenomena," 157

Status: expression of anger and, 204–205; skill at deciphering nonverbal messages related to, 92–93; Space Rules, Power, and Status exercise on, 115–119; touch implications for workplace, 109. *See also* Power

Stereotyping: about sex differences in speech communication, 37–47; of gender communication differences, 15; of sex-role perceptions and expectations, 27

The Strong Silent Type exercise, 128–130

Suspending judgment disclaimer, 56

T

Tag questions, 54–56

Take Charge! slide, 244

Talk Remedies for Communication Between Men and Women (full-day program): description and theme of, 289; Objectives slide on, 295; outline and activities of, 290–294

Talk Remedies for Communication Between Men and Women (half-day program): description and theme of, 276; Objectives slide of, 279; outline and activities of, 276–279

Talk Remedies for Communication Between Men and Women (one-hour program): description and theme of, 267; handouts for, 269; outline and activities of, 267–268; talk remedies and objectives slides for, 269

Tannen, D., 35, 43–44, 61, 68, 179, 187

Thomas, Kenneth W., 301, 303

Thomas-Kilmann Conflict Mode Instrument (TKI), 211, 301–303

Thompson, W., 206

Tingley, J., 26, 44–45, 160, 263

Todd, Z., 226

Todorov, A., 111–112

Topics: female tendency toward "troubles-talk," 44; male focus on "safe," 44–45; male tendency to select the, 42

Touch, Power, and Perceived Power exercise, 105–109

Touching: appropriate or inappropriate, 102; Her and His First Impressions exercise on, 110–115; Learning Gender Touch: Touch the Girl and Not the Boy exercise on, 101–105; nonverbal communication through, 90; Touch, Power, and Perceived Power exercise on, 105–109

Training programs: additional instruments and training tools for, 297–304; closing the, 242–261; Evaluation Form, 304; full-day programs, 281–295; half-day programs, 271–280. *See also* Exercises and slides; Handouts

"Troubles-talk," 44

Turn taking, 67, 72, 76

U

Uhlmann, E. L., 204

Unspoken gender messages: Behaviors That Are "On" or "Off" the Record exercise on, 96–98; Case Study: Something in the Way She Feels exercise on, 99–101; double messages and, 93–95, 189–190; Find Meaning in What You Don't Say exercise on, 88–93; Nonverbal Communication slide on, 90

U.S. culture: on fair fighting, 212; gender differences in workplace power in the, 108; space and distance indicators of gender power/status in, 117–118

U.S. Senate study, 205